the LEAN CFO

ARCHITECT OF THE LEAN MANAGEMENT SYSTEM

the LEAN CFO

ARCHITECT OF THE LEAN MANAGEMENT SYSTEM

Nicholas S. Katko

CRC Press
Taylor & Francis Group
Boca Raton London New York

CRC Press is an imprint of the
Taylor & Francis Group, an **informa** business

A PRODUCTIVITY PRESS BOOK

CRC Press
Taylor & Francis Group
6000 Broken Sound Parkway NW, Suite 300
Boca Raton, FL 33487-2742

Printed on acid-free paper
Version Date: 20130424

International Standard Book Number-13: 978-1-4665-9940-6 (Hardback)

Library of Congress Cataloging-in-Publication Data

Katko, Nicholas S.
The lean CFO : architect of the lean management system / Nicholas S. Katko.
pages cm
Includes bibliographical references and index.
ISBN 978-1-4665-9940-6 (alk. paper)
1. Cost control. 2. Chief financial officers. I. Title.

HD47.3.K37 2013
658.15'52--dc23   2013015179

Visit the Taylor & Francis Web site at
http://www.taylorandfrancis.com

and the CRC Press Web site at
http://www.crcpress.com

Contents

Preface

I began my CFO career working for an established manufacturing company that had been around for many years. Manufacturing practices and financial analysis related to operations were pretty standard and established.

Soon our company made the commitment to become Lean. We hired people with Lean experience. Talk about continuous improvement, flow, and eliminating waste all seemed foreign to me, something that "the Lean people" would work on. But pretty soon these "Lean people" were coming to me and asking for different kinds of financial work, such as performance measures and financial analysis not using standard costs. Boy, was I out of my comfort zone!

Over time, with the help and support of the "Lean people," I figured out how Lean could make us a lot of money. Then I was all in on Lean. Every improvement I had to make and every new type of analysis I had to do suddenly all made sense. I began thinking of myself as one of the "Lean people": the Lean CFO.

And in my work with our customers in BMA, Inc., I've consistently talked about the unique role the CFO has in leading a company down its Lean journey by becoming a Lean CFO. The more I talked about the role and responsibilities of the Lean CFO, the more I developed a coherent message.

Then my colleague, Brian Maskell, suggested that I write a book. That got me out of my comfort zone, just like Lean did many years ago. Talking about it is one thing, but having to sit down and write about it is another. To write this book, I've had to adjust my thinking and break down my internal paradigms of not being able to write a book. It was no different for me than figuring out how Lean makes money.

Even though the book is titled *The Lean CFO,* it is really intended for financial people, business executives, and Lean leaders. It doesn't matter if your company is just getting started with Lean or has been Lean for years. There is something in it for everybody.

This book is not about debits, credits, or accounting theory. It's about how a CFO becomes a Lean CFO by leading a company in developing and deploying a Lean Management System.

I hope that you enjoy the book and find it useful.

Acknowledgments

THANKS TO...

My wife, Deanna Katko, who has been very supportive of my writing this book, knowing I needed time to think and write. She has been an excellent sounding board for my ideas and always responded with excellent comments. Finally, she has supported my career at Brian Maskell Associates (BMA), which requires me to travel all the time and leaves her to manage things while I'm away in addition to running her own business.

Justin Katko, who made the time while completing his dissertation to read and edit this book. It's good to have a son who holds a PhD in English.

Ritchie Katko and Molly Buchenberger, who helped me formulate the theme of the book around the architecture process and helped with illustrations. It's also good to have a son who is a landscape architect and a daughter-in-law who is an architect.

Brian Maskell and Bruce Baggaley, who took a chance on hiring me into BMA, Inc., 11 years ago. It's been great working with them and learning from them. Thanks to them for giving me this opportunity and allowing me to develop my own voice.

Susan Lilly, who guided me through the book development process. She helped me create the illustrations and handled all the technical aspects of preparing this book for publication.

All the great people with whom I have worked helping their companies implement Lean accounting. Every experience has been a learning experience for me and has played a part in creating this book.

And The Boss, for keeping me inspired while writing.

The Author

After a tour of duty in public accounting, **Nick Katko** began his Lean management system career as chief financial officer of Bullard, a privately held manufacturing company in Kentucky.

In the mid-1990s Bullard made a commitment to a Lean business strategy and began hiring operations people with Lean experience. Nick worked with Lean leaders to establish a comprehensive Lean performance measurement system that was used to measure and manage the entire business.

As inventory was dramatically reduced, Nick realized the irrelevance of the standard costing system to the business. Nick created and introduced value stream income statements to Bullard, and all business decision making was based upon a value stream financial analysis of decisions. Eventually, labor and overhead rates were set to zero and inventory valuation was made with a simple monthly journal entry capitalizing manufacturing costs.

In 2000, Nick left Bullard and started Strategic Financial Solutions, Inc., with his wife Deanna. Strategic Financial Solutions provides contract CFO and controller services as well as bookkeeping and tax services to companies in the Lexington, Kentucky area.

While on Bullard's Lean journey, Nick read *Making the Numbers Count* by Brian Maskell. He liked the book so much he wrote Brian and told him about his own work with a Lean Management System. Nick and Brian talked regularly and, in 2002, Brian asked Nick to join BMA, Inc., as a senior consultant.

As a senior consultant with BMA, Nick uses his experience to assist clients in Lean management implementation by working closely with them to resolve the real-world issues they face in implementation. These issues include removing traditional cost-based performance measurement systems in favor of Lean performance measurement systems, migrating from a traditional income statement to a value stream costing income statement, creating a transaction elimination maturity path, and working with management to create new business decision-making models based on Lean accounting practices.

Nick has worked with a wide range of businesses, from multinational public companies to family-owned businesses around the world. He is the co-author of *The Lean Business Management System: Lean Accounting Principles and Practices Toolkit* (2007) as well as the BMA Lean Accounting Webinar Series. He is a regular presenter at the Lean Accounting Summit and the Lean Enterprise China Summit.

Nick, a native of Sayreville, New Jersey, resides in Lexington, Kentucky with his wife, Deanna, and family. He holds a BS in accounting and an MBA in finance, both from the University of Kentucky, and is a certified public accountant.

Nick has set up a website (www.theleancfo.com) to create an interactive learning experience to accompany reading this book. As you read the book, use the website to ask Nick questions, share your stories, raise issues in a forum, and get the latest from The Lean CFO Blog.

1

The Architect

INTRODUCTION

As a chief financial officer, you are responsible for an external financial reporting system as well as an internal management accounting system. Your financial reporting system is regulated by generally accepted accounting principles (GAAP) and your responsibility is to produce GAAP-compliant financial statements. The primary reason for this is so that external users of your financial statements can fairly assess and understand your company's financial condition.

On the other hand, management uses a management accounting system to control business operations and to make sound financial business decisions. As a CFO, you are the architect of your company's management accounting system. It needs to be designed around the operating practices of your company so that it meets the needs of management.

Figure 1.1 illustrates the typical management accounting system for a traditional manufacturing company. In traditional manufacturing, operations are controlled by measuring against a production plan. Inventory must also be controlled because there is so much of it, which has a material impact on financial reporting. Business decision making focused on improving efficiencies and absorption, as well as lowering the cost of inventory, is viewed favorably. So this management accounting system is entirely appropriate in this manufacturing environment.

Lean companies have a completely different operating control environment, which is pretty much 100% opposite of traditional manufacturing. As seen in Figure 1.2, Lean companies control production by producing to demand and creating flow. Business decisions that improve delivering value and productivity will drive profitable growth.

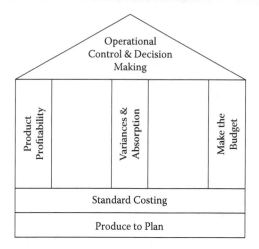

FIGURE 1.1
Traditional management accounting system.

The day your company adopts Lean, you face an immediate challenge: You must be the architect of a Lean Management System to replace your current management accounting system. Like an architect, you must design the Lean Management System and manage its construction. After it is constructed, you must literally "move" your company into the new system and then demolish the old management accounting system.

To create the Lean Management System for your company, you must transform yourself from a CFO into a Lean CFO. This book provides you

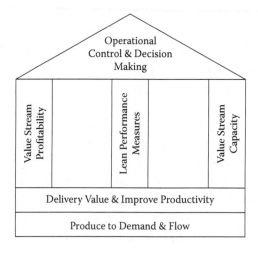

FIGURE 1.2
Lean Management System.

with the blueprint that explains how to become a Lean CFO and build a Lean Management System.

DESIGNING THE LEAN MANAGEMENT SYSTEM

During the design phase of a project, an architect works with the client to agree on the functional requirements, layout, and sustainability of the structure based on the client's needs.

The functional requirement of a Lean Management System is to drive Lean forward and achieve financial success. Ask people what "Lean" means and you will get many different answers. But it is at least one thing: a proven money-making strategy. Lean will make your company money if its principles are followed, its practices executed as intended, and the proper measures are in place.

Chapter 2, "The Economics of Lean," explains the strategic aspects of making money from a Lean business strategy. Lean principles, practices, and tools can be very confusing to people, and companies, without prior Lean experience. This chapter explains how the combination of Lean principles, practices, and tools changes the laws of supply and demand for your company. Lean will do two things for your company: drive it to create more value for your customers and continuously improve your productivity. Creating more value for customers drives revenue growth; improving productivity drives cost management, which results in increasing profits as Lean matures. The economics of Lean is your mantra as the Lean CFO.

The operational execution of Lean can be summarized in one word: Flow. The creation, maintenance, and improvement of flow will unlock the financial potential of Lean for your company. Chapter 3, "$how Me the Value Stream Flow," discusses how flow increases operating profit and lays the foundation for why your company's entire measurement system must change. Chapter 4, "$how Me the Office Flow," discusses how office flow can drive the financial success of Lean by putting Lean practices into place in every process in your business.

As the Lean CFO, you don't need to be an expert in implementing flow. You do need to develop a good understanding of the relationships between Lean operations, Lean measurements, and financial statements that will allow you to design the Lean Management System.

CONSTRUCTING THE LEAN MANAGEMENT SYSTEM

After completing the design, the next job of the architect is to supervise and manage the proper construction of the structure. You must make sure the construction is done according to the design specifications.

The design specs of the Lean Management System are summarized in the Box Score (Figure 1.3): the combination of performance measures, value stream accounting, and value stream capacity, all of which drive Lean performance forward throughout the organization. Entirely new systems must be constructed to produce this information.

Chapter 5, "Measure Performance, Not Profits," explains how and why you must move your company away from performance measures based on traditional manufacturing practices and into a Lean performance measurement system. New measures must be created that support flow, continuous improvement, problem solving, and creating value. The Lean performance measurement system is essential to the success of Lean. Traditional performance measures just won't work.

			Current State	Future State	
Operational		Sales per Person	$7,472	$7,472	Performance measures reflect improvements as waste is eliminated
		On-Time Shipment	92%	94%	
		First Time Through	71%	78%	
		Doc-to-Doc Days	33.0	18.5	
		Average Cost	$419.46	$413.97	
Capacity	Machines Employees	Productive	51%	43%	Eliminating waste transforms non-productive capacity into available capacity
		Nonproductive	30%	19%	
		Available Capacity	19%	37%	
		Productive	53%	53%	
		Nonproductive	32%	17%	
		Available Capacity	15%	29%	
Financial		Revenue	$332.569	$332,569	Value stream income statement measures profitability by value stream
		Material Costs	$111,431	$108,446	
		Conversion Costs	$116,753	$116,753	
		Total Costs	$228,184	$225,199	
		Value Stream Profit	$104,385	$107,370	
		Return on Sales	31%	32%	
		Inventory Value	$209,336	$113,026	
		Cash Flow	$123,117	$288,926	

FIGURE 1.3
Box Score example.

Chapter 6, "It's about Spending, Not Costs," describes how you must move your company into value stream accounting, which simply reports your internal financial information by the real profit centers of your business, your value streams. Value stream profit is simply the difference between what a value stream ships and how much it spends—no standard costing, no complex cost allocations.

Lean companies recognize that the primary root cause of costs is based on spending decisions. As the Lean CFO, you need to move the emphasis of financial analysis away from a few accountants analyzing costs to the entire company constantly managing spending. This is accomplished by giving people in the company what they really need: information on how much they are spending. Combining spending reports with Lean problem-solving practices will lead to lower costs.

Chapter 7, "The Value of Measuring Capacity," explains why you construct a value stream capacity measurement system. Lean companies look at their people and machines as resources—not as operating expenses. These resources have capacity, which can be used for productive activities such as producing customer demand, or for nonproductive activities such as rework, defects, downtime, and other waste. Capacity usage must be measured from a Lean viewpoint—not from a traditional viewpoint such as standard hours.

As the Lean CFO, you must lead the effort to measure capacity to drive the economics of Lean into your company's decision making. Using Lean practices to eliminate waste will create capacity, and there will be many business decisions that have to be made about how to use that capacity. The ultimate financial outcome of these business decisions will be dependent on the accuracy of this capacity information.

MOVING INTO LEAN BUSINESS DECISION MAKING

You've designed and constructed the Lean Management System. Now it's time to move your company into it. This means using it throughout the business to manage every facet of your Lean business.

In many manufacturing companies, standard cost information is still the predominant source of information used to analyze operations and make business decisions. This is dangerous for a Lean company, because standard costing is designed for, and works quite well in, mass-production manufacturing. But Lean is an operating system that is totally incommensurate with mass production. Continuing to make business decisions using standard costing in a Lean company will lead to conflict and confusion.

In order for a Lean business strategy to lead to financial success, the Lean CFO must remove standard costing from all business decisions. Business decision methods in Lean companies need to be aligned with the economics of Lean. The companies must understand the financial impact of decisions based on (a) how demand is changed due to creating customer value, and (b) how spending is changed due to operational and capacity improvements. Chapter 8 illustrates how to make many typical business decisions using the Box Score.

TEARING DOWN THE OLD HOUSE

Your final job as architect of the Lean Management System is to tear down the old management accounting system. There is no reason for keeping it, because it is now obsolete. No one lives in the old house anymore, and you don't want anyone trying to move back into it.

Chapter 9, "Standard Costing Debunked," explains how to break your company away from using standard costing to run the business. Standard costing is the foundation of most management accounting systems in traditional manufacturing companies. The reason for this is inventory. When a company has lots of inventory, the production and valuation of that inventory has a material impact on financial reporting. Standard costing works quite well in this environment.

A Lean company does not need any information from a standard costing system to run or manage its business. The Lean Management System is what is used. A Lean company may need standard costing early in its Lean journey temporarily to do one thing: value inventory. The reason that this is only done temporarily is that Lean will dramatically reduce inventory. And once inventory is reduced, its valuation is no longer material for financial reporting.

As the Lean CFO, you must first develop a plan to simplify standard costing so that you can still use it for inventory valuation, but not let it interfere with Lean operations. Once inventory is reduced, standard costing must be eliminated. Chapter 9 explains exactly how to develop such a plan for your company.

Chapter 10, "Tame the ERP Beast," explains how and why your ERP (enterprise resource planning) system must be modified to support Lean rather than hinder it. ERP systems are designed for traditional manufacturing practices and can gather and report as much information as you have designed them to do. Lean operations rely on performance measurements and visual signals to manage and control production. A Lean factory has little reliance on ERP. If your ERP system is not modified, it will impede flow, because operations will be required to enter many unnecessary transactions, which will produce unnecessary information and reports, all of which is waste. Because you have a vested interest in your company's ERP system, which feeds your general ledger, you must work with operations and your information technology people to develop and create a plan to simplify ERP.

That is a summary of your blueprint. Now let's get started on the Lean Management System.

2

The Economics of Lean

INTRODUCTION

The first question I always ask when I begin a seminar or an event with a company is: "What is Lean?" I ask everyone to say whatever comes to their mind and always get a wide variety of responses. This simple exercise demonstrates that Lean usually means different things to people, and the common thread to their responses is that people usually answer the question based on their role in the company or the department in which they work. One of the keys to financial success with Lean is that it has to mean the same thing to everyone in the company.

LEAN IS THE STRATEGY

To achieve financial success with Lean, it must be *the* strategy of your company. Some companies understand this, but many companies think Lean is "part" of a business strategy. This distinction may not seem that important, but it has a dramatic impact on what a company thinks it can accomplish with Lean.

If a company thinks Lean is "part" of a business strategy, then it will selectively implement certain Lean practices. The usual approach in these companies is to think that Lean applies strictly to operations, with a desire to cut costs. The end result is that there may be some improvements made in operations, but for the most part, it's business as usual.

Lean is a business strategy that impacts every part of the company. Every person, from the CEO to the shop floor operator, from the marketing manager to the accounting clerk, will have to change the way he or she thinks about and does his or her work. Every business process will be analyzed the same way and rebuilt to better serve its customers. Adopting Lean practices, tools, and methods cannot be avoided. Excuses such as "Lean doesn't apply to us" or "we are different" are not acceptable.

LEAN EVERY DAY

Companies that adopt a Lean business strategy are successful because they employ Lean practices every day, everywhere, all the time. On a daily basis, the Lean company focuses on three things: (1) delivering value to its customers, (2) flowing all business processes, and (3) relentlessly eliminating waste. Success with Lean is dependent on how it is executed on a daily basis (Figure 2.1).

Lean is often called a journey because it takes time, effort, and discipline to establish daily Lean practices throughout the business. Every business process must be transformed into a customer-focused process. Continuous improvement must become part of everyone's job. The entire culture of the company must be changed. And all of this must be done while you are also trying to run the business.

"Lean Every Day" is a monumental task and often competes with other management initiatives in companies. This is something to avoid. Since Lean is the strategy, all Lean initiatives need to take priority over non-Lean initiatives to achieve true financial success.

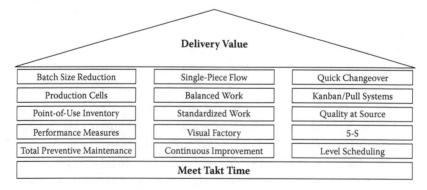

FIGURE 2.1
Operations built on Lean practices.

THE ECONOMICS OF LEAN

The economics of Lean can be explained in basic terms of supply and demand (Figure 2.2). Let's look at demand first. By focusing on creating and delivering customer value, the demand for your company's products or services increases and you command better prices. Financially, this means the growth rate of your revenue should increase compared to your historical growth rate and should be better than industry averages.

The supply side of the equation focuses on your supply of resources. Your supply of people, machines, and facilities is responsible for creating and delivering customer value. By focusing on creating flow and continuous improvement, the productivity of your resources will improve dramatically. Using Lean practices to create flow means that resources will be able to maintain productivity levels regardless of short-term fluctuations in demand. Continuous improvement practices will allow your company to realize annual productivity improvements of 15–20%.

The financial impact of maintaining and improving your resources' productivity is that the rate of increase in the cost of those resources (i.e., your operating expenses) will slow down and be less than the growth rate of

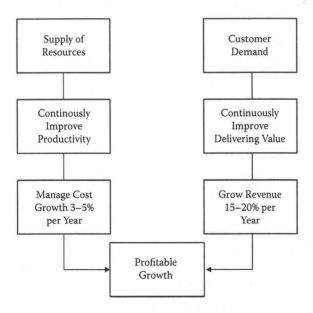

FIGURE 2.2
The economics of Lean.

your revenue. The difference in growth rates between revenue and costs means your company will make tons of money with Lean.

Sounds easy, right? Everything about Lean sounds easy, but it's hard to do because a company is basically working against itself when it comes to becoming Lean. It takes a great deal of discipline to break away from traditional thinking, daily fire fighting, and the inertia to keep doing things the same way. It's about human nature. The comfort of the known, the current state of business processes, and all the problems that go along with them are more acceptable than totally different business processes that obliterate your current way of thinking.

Fortunately, there is a solution: measures. A key to financial success with Lean is measuring based on how Lean works. As the CFO, you are the resident expert on measurements.

THE LEAN CFO—KEY TO SUCCESS WITH LEAN

So where does the CFO fit into all of this? As CFO, you chart the financial strategy of your company. Whatever the business strategy, you need to project the financial impact of the proper execution of the strategy. You also have oversight of the management accounting system: the measures and methods that are used internally to measure how well a company is performing at any time. How you present the financial benefit of Lean and how you determine how to measure it will be the determining factors of whether a company adopts Lean as *the* business strategy or thinks of Lean as "part" of a business strategy.

As the Lean CFO, you need to understand the economics of Lean so that you can align your financial strategy with how Lean makes a company money. You need to make the necessary changes to financial measurement and reporting systems to measure the execution of the Lean business strategy. I believe this is the single most important factor that prevents companies from realizing the true financial potential of Lean. Your ability to translate the language of Lean into the language of money will make it clear to everyone in your business why the proper implementation and daily execution of Lean practices are necessary.

It is very important for you to change the financial and operational measurement system so that the measures drive Lean behaviors. Traditional measures, of course, will drive traditional behaviors. That is what they are designed to do. But these traditional measures will obscure and undermine the vital changes required by the economics of Lean.

FIVE LEAN PRINCIPLES

The economics of Lean are based on the five principles of Lean: customer value, value streams, flow and pull, pursue perfection, and empower employees (Figure 2.3). Adopting a Lean business strategy means these principles become the way of life for your company. These principles permeate the entire organization: its cultures, operating practices, and management style. Let's take a look at how these principles impact measuring and reporting.

The number one objective of a Lean business strategy is to provide value to your customers and to your markets. This requires two things. First, a company must clearly understand value *from the customer's perspective.* Second, it must *actually deliver* the exact value the customers want. By doing both, a company will change the dynamics of its relationships between itself, its customers, and its competition. These are the reasons

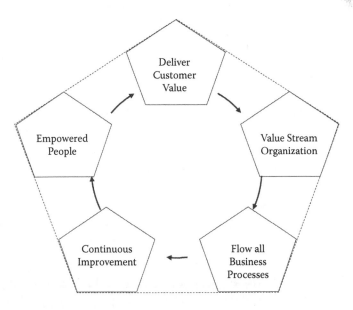

FIGURE 2.3
The five principles of Lean.

why measurement and reporting systems need to be changed. You need to measure how well any operation delivers customer value, at any time.

What exactly is value and how is it delivered? It's easy to identify when you look at the products or services your customers buy. These products or services must meet certain quality specifications and delivery standards. Lean companies understand that value is more than just the product or service. Customer value is created every time a customer has an encounter with your company. Think of all the encounters your customers have with your company outside the actual use of your product or service. Placing an order, receiving and paying the invoice, after-sales support, navigating your website, and the ease of talking to a person in your company are just some examples of where value can be created. This is the reason Lean companies identify, organize, and manage by value streams.

The second principle of Lean is working by value streams. Value streams are not departments (Figure 2.4a–c). A value stream is the sequence of process steps from the time a customer places an order to the time the customer receives the product or service, executed at the proper time. Value streams are the profit centers of your business. These are the reasons why measurement and management systems need to be aligned around value streams, because the only way to increase profitability is for value stream performance to improve. All financial and operational measurements must be changed to focus on the performance of value streams.

Before I go on, let me explain a subtle, but important, difference between value streams and business processes. Value streams focus on order fulfillment: meeting customer demand and generating revenue. Business processes also meet customer demand, but they do not generate revenue. As I mentioned previously, Lean is a comprehensive business strategy that impacts the entire organization, not just the factory. Throughout this book I will be using the term "value streams," but everything written about value streams applies equally to every business process.

The responsibility of the Lean CFO is to change measurement systems so that the delivery of value can be measured consistently and frequently throughout the entire business. Every business process delivers

> **Value stream definition:** the actions taken, in the proper sequence, at the proper time, to create value for some customer and the information required for coordinating these actions.

Traditional Organizational Structure

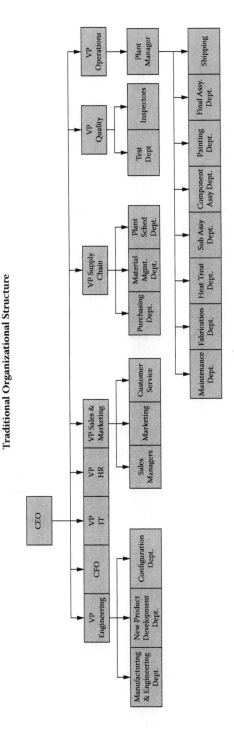

FIGURE 2.4(a)

A traditional organizational structure.

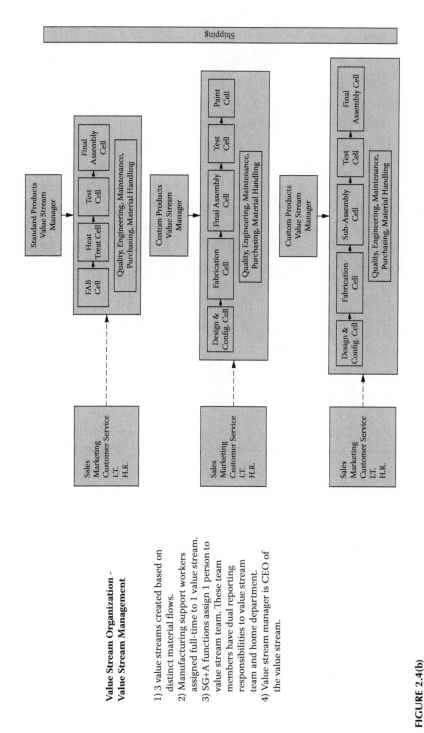

Value Stream Organization - Value Stream Management

1) 3 value streams created based on distinct material flows.
2) Manufacturing support workers assigned full-time to 1 value stream.
3) SG+A functions assign 1 person to value stream team. These team members have dual reporting responsibilities to value stream team and home department.
4) Value stream manager is CEO of the value stream.

FIGURE 2.4(b)
Value stream organization—value stream management.

Value Stream Organization – Corporate Structure

Corporate departments do not totally disappear in a value stream organization. Small teams of functional experts are responsible for setting strategic direction of company in areas such as quality and procurement. This execution of that strategy resides at the value stream level with the value stream team.

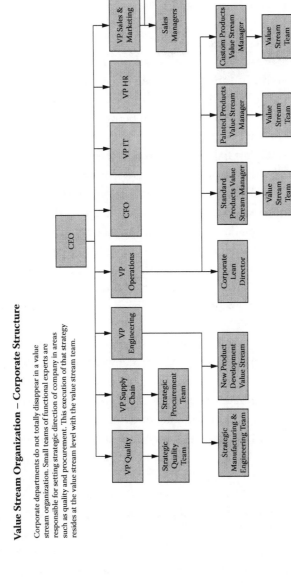

FIGURE 2.4(c)

Value stream organization—corporate structure.

Value streams must win over departments. You must take specific steps in your organization to make sure that the existing departmental reporting structure doesn't undermine value stream management.

value. Value streams create and deliver value to your paying customers. Internally, other business processes deliver value to internal customers or other stakeholders. Every business process needs the same basic measures.

Lean companies recognize that their supply of resources creates and delivers customer value. A company's resources are its people, machines, and facilities. These resources work in the value streams and other business processes. The number one objective for every value stream is to maximize the amount of time it spends on creating customer value. The primary issue is that every value stream and every business process contains waste, and waste prevents value from being created.

Lean companies want every value stream to do two things very well, all the time: Flow (principle #3) demands through the value stream as quickly as possible and relentlessly eliminates waste (principle #4). In order to accomplish these two objectives, value streams need to be able to manage flow and waste. This requires a fundamental change in the measurement of operations. Measuring flow and waste will result in tremendous gains in productivity. The Lean CFO must quickly move the company away from traditional cost-based measurement systems in the early stages of Lean. It's vital that everyone in the organization learns quickly how to execute a Lean business strategy properly, and the best way to do this is with new measurements.

For a Lean strategy to work, everybody, everywhere, all the time focuses on creating value (Figure 2.5). This is the principle of empowering employees. The primary objective is for people to take action: to deliver value, improve flow, and eliminate waste. Lean measurement and management systems need to focus on actions and outcomes, not simply reporting numbers. This means that these systems need to be simple and easy for everyone. The right information needs to be reported as frequently as necessary to ensure that the right actions are being taken. Measurement and management systems need to be redesigned with the users—every employee—in mind. The traditional approach to measurement and management systems is to increase the dependence on ERP (enterprise resource planning) systems. Lean takes the opposite approach and the Lean CFO

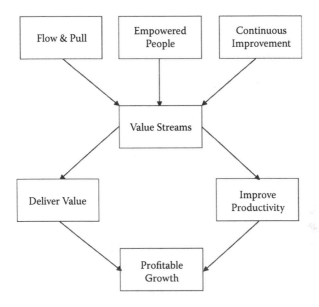

FIGURE 2.5
Linking Lean principles to the economics of Lean.

needs to lead the company away from complex measurement systems that no one understands to Lean-focused measurement systems.

WRAP-UP

The economics of Lean form the foundation for all the changes that need to be made by the Lean CFO. There is a tremendous amount of money to be made from a Lean business strategy, but most people can't see this because existing measurement and management systems are not designed with Lean economics in mind. The Lean CFO must redesign all measurement and reporting systems to unlock the financial potential of Lean.

3

$how Me the Value Stream Flow

INTRODUCTION

As a CFO you are given a business case and asked: "How much money will be made from this?" The outcome of the decision rests with your financial analysis. How would you, as CFO, answer this question about Lean? Your answer depends on your perspective of Lean.

It's common knowledge that Lean eliminates waste. The issue is how to measure what Lean does. A traditionally thinking company measures waste elimination by the amount of labor time saved. The traditionally thinking CFO's financial analysis is quite simple. Multiply the total labor time saved by a labor rate to get the total savings Lean will generate. Often the cost saving will be claimed but the number of employees does not change and no spending has really been reduced. Or people are laid off based on these "Lean" improvements and the Lean journey stops because people will not work on "improvements" that take their jobs away. In addition, this traditional perspective totally ignores the impact on revenue of improving the delivery of customer value by your company.

In Chapter 2 we learned that part of the financial success with Lean occurs if a company can continuously improve productivity. Productivity improvements do not simply come from randomly eliminating waste. Value Streams need to be redesigned to emphasize creating customer value above all else. The redesign of value streams to improve the delivery of customer value is known as flow, the third principle of Lean. Real improvement in productivity occurs when flow systems are established in every value stream and administrative process in a company. The responsibility of the Lean CFO is to create a measurement system that measures and manages flow.

WHAT IS FLOW?

Flow is probably the hardest part of becoming a truly Lean company. First, establishing flow requires "system thinking": The entire value stream needs to work in a coordinated manner always to meet exact, specific customer needs and maintain productivity levels no matter how demand fluctuates. This requires everyone working in a value stream to have a good understanding of customer needs as well as understanding the relationships between the process steps in the value stream (Figures 3.1 and 3.2).

Second, establishing flow requires a redesign of the processes so that it works according to Lean practices; It doesn't just require the simple elimination of random waste. Once flow is established, it must be constantly monitored and measured so that interruptions to flow are quickly discovered and addressed. Also, maintaining flow requires a constant measuring and managing of the process by the people that work in that process.

Finally, sequence of all the value-added as well as necessary work required from receipt of an order to delivery of the product must be done at the proper time. The value stream includes the value-added production process steps to transform the raw materials into a finished product as well as all other **necessary activities** required to support these value-added process steps. This means that the work of quality, maintenance, engineering, scheduling, purchasing, and material management (collectively known as "indirect labor") is part of your company's value streams. If these necessary activities aren't undertaken at the proper times, then value stream flow is interrupted.

Lean companies determine how to incorporate these activities into value streams so that they do no inhibit flow. The old departmental silos are another form of waste, totally created by your organization structure. It's pretty easy to eliminate it, since you created it. There are three ways to eliminate this waste: Move the manufacturing support people into the value stream; move the work into the value stream; or pull the support resources to value streams based on demand. Figure 3.3 summarizes the various Lean practices used to eliminate the waste of manufacturing support departments.

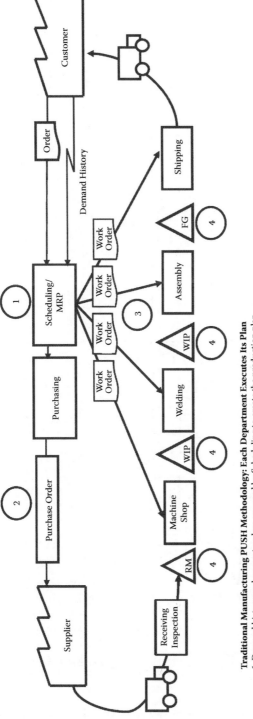

Traditional Manufacturing PUSH Methodology: Each Department Executes Its Plan

1. Demand history and current orders are used by Scheduling to create the production plan
2. Purchasing receives a purchase forecast from MRP and is responsible for buying materials according to the plan
3. Each manufacturing department receives work orders from MRP and is responsible for executing the production plan
4. The result: inventory

FIGURE 3.1

Traditional manufacturing.

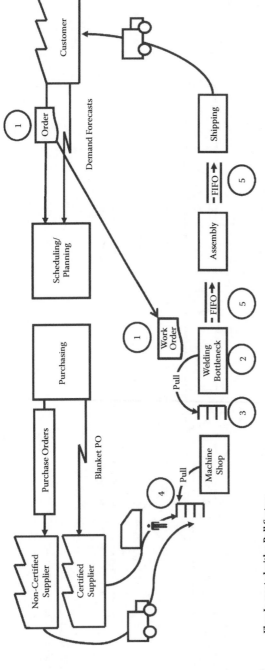

Flow Is created with a Pull System

1. Production is based on actual demand, not on an MRP-generated forecast

2. Every value stream has a bottleneck – i.e., the process step with the longest cycle time – and this is the only step which needs to be scheduled. Welding is the bottleneck process in this value stream.

3. A supermarket is created between machining and welding to regulate the work of machining, so it matches the rate of work in welding. Machining will replenish this supermarket at the rate that Welding pulls.

4. A pull system is established between machining and suppliers. Machining signals suppliers when its inventory needs to be replenished. The supplier delivers at regular intervals.

5. Because assembly works faster than welding, it produces one-at-a time as welding completes it work. Then the finished product is flowed directly to shipping for delivery to the customer.

The result: dramatic reduction of inventory.

FIGURE 3.2

Flow created with pull system.

Function	Traditional practice	Waste created	Lean practice
Quality	Inspectors	1. Waiting time 2. Inventory 3. Longer lead times	Quality at source: 1. Operator standard work 2. Inspectors assigned to value stream or 3. Pull inspectors to value stream by visual signal
Maintenance	Scheduling and planning software	1. Excessive downtime 2. Schedule adherence	1. Total preventive maintenance by operators 2. Assign maintenance people to value stream 3. Single piece flow of maintenance work orders based on value stream demand
Procurement	Centralized purchasing using MRP	1. Inventory 2. Poor on-time delivery	1. Kanban pull from cells to supplier with delivery direct to the cell 2. Certified suppliers with daily delivery
Planning and scheduling	MRP production planning	1. Inventory 2. Poor on-time delivery 3. Expediting	1. Visual pull systems 2. Schedule bottleneck process based on demand 3. MRP used for high-level planning only

FIGURE 3.3

Eliminating manufacturing support waste.

FLOW EQUALS REAL PRODUCTIVITY

The ultimate goal of Lean is single piece flow, which simply means working on one product at a time from start to finish before beginning to work on the next product. If each process step in a value stream achieves single piece flow, then the entire value stream achieves single piece flow.

The reality is that pure single piece flow is difficult to do because of variability that exists in processes. There are three types of variability that exist in all value streams: the variability of demand, the variability of cycle times, and the variability of waste. Lean practices either eliminate or manage the variability. There are of course many causes of variability, and there is no "silver bullet" that solves them. Variability is removed by constant monitoring of the process by the operators, who identify continuous improvement opportunities. Continuous improvement gradually addresses the root causes of variability in a systematic, disciplined manner. The result is not just a quick fix, but permanent resolution of the problems.

Establishing flow is the first step to achieving productivity gains. Just as the CFO oversees internal control systems to ensure that the financial numbers are valid and relevant, the Lean CFO must oversee the Lean data collection and measurement systems to ensure that these numbers are also valid and relevant. The numbers are used to identify waste, drive continuous improvement, measure progress, and ensure that solutions are sustained over time. The result is genuine productivity gains.

ELIMINATE WASTE AND IMPROVE FLOW

Waste must be eliminated to improve flow. Continuous improvement systems identify and eliminate waste. Companies design processes that contain waste, but they can eliminate the waste if a measurement system is designed to reveal waste and manage flow.

Before waste can be eliminated, it first must be measured. The waste in any value stream is measured when mapping the current state of the value stream. This is a critical step in continuous improvement, because if the waste is not measured properly, then kaizen events will not be effective in removing it.

As the Lean CFO you do not need to become an expert in value stream mapping; however, you do need to ensure that the data collection process used to create the current-state map is objective and valid, and that the right measures are in place to show the flow and the waste.

The recommended method of measuring waste in the current state is direct observation of the process. We're not talking about 6-month time studies. We are talking about people observing the process as it is working and noting the time spent on all wasteful activities. For statistically valid data, about thirty observations are needed. The types and amount of waste observed will guide the continuous improvement efforts. These observations are an essential part of Lean thinking, known as "going to the gemba." This approach derives from the understanding that you have to see and experience the problems firsthand if you wish to truly understand them. Studies and computer-based analysis might be helpful, but true learning only comes from direct observation.

These observations often focus on the "Seven Wastes" that were classified by one of the originators of Lean methods, Mr. Shigeo Shingo. These wastes include:

- Transportation
- Human motion
- Defects and inspection
- Inventory
- Overproduction
- Waiting
- Overprocessing

 7 wastes

The end result of observing the value stream is data collection boxes on value stream maps (Figure 3.4), which summarize waste such as:

- Scrap and rework rates
- Wait time of products between process steps
- Downtime of people or machines
- Amount of time spent getting parts, tools, and any other activity other than adding value to the product
- Changeover time of machines

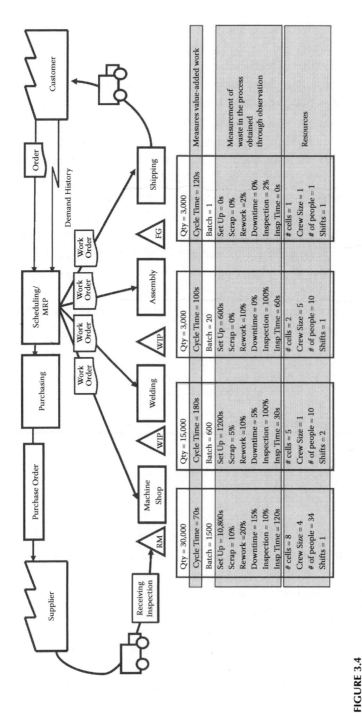

FIGURE 3.4
Value stream map and data boxes.

DEMAND AND CYCLE TIMES IMPACT FLOW

It is typically more difficult to eliminate the variability of demand and cycle times, so this variability is managed. The combination of Lean practices used to manage the variability is known as "pull systems."

The overall level of demand, such as incoming orders, can vary significantly over short periods of time. Additionally, the product mix of demand creates further variability. Finally, the cycle times to do the work in each process step are not the same. Eliminating this variability can be difficult and costly.

To manage this variability, pull systems are established. Pull systems include various Lean practices and tools used to level-load the demand and regulate the work between process steps to create single piece flow. These methods include quick changeover, kanban or other visual signals, standard work, balanced work, identification of the bottleneck operation, and the "stop the line and fix the problem" method known as "Andon."

The Lean CFO must work with the Lean team to ensure that demand and cycle times are measured accurately and consistently throughout the organization. Demand is measured as takt time, which is simply the level of demand as measured in time, not units (Figure 3.5a, b). Takt time is the total minutes in a month divided by the average demand in a month. This is the average time interval that a unit of demand needs to be produced. Lean companies measure demand in takt time so that it can be compared to the total cycle time, which is the rate at which a product can be produced. flow is achieved and proven to work when the total cycle time is around 80% of average takt time. The "80% rule" allows for a smooth and consistent flow of production. Poor measurements of demand and cycle times will largely eliminate the effectiveness of continuous improvement activities. It is also essential to have well designed, simple, and visual measurements throughout the entire value stream so that the value stream is always under control and true flow is achieved.

LEAN PERFORMANCE MEASUREMENTS

For flow to achieve productivity gains, Lean performance measurements are required. Furthermore, traditional measures that are not Lean focused

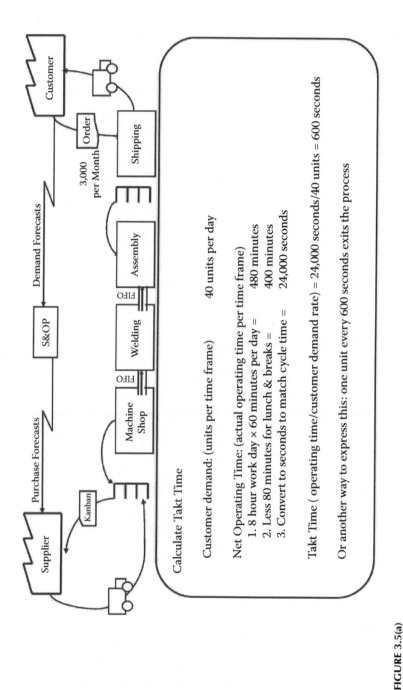

Calculate Takt Time

Customer demand: (units per time frame)   40 units per day

Net Operating Time: (actual operating time per time frame)
1. 8 hour work day × 60 minutes per day =   480 minutes
2. Less 80 minutes for lunch & breaks =   400 minutes
3. Convert to seconds to match cycle time =   24,000 seconds

Takt Time (operating time/customer demand rate) = 24,000 seconds/40 units = 600 seconds

Or another way to express this: one unit every 600 seconds exits the process

FIGURE 3.5(a)
Understanding how takt time and cycle time affect flow.

n♭

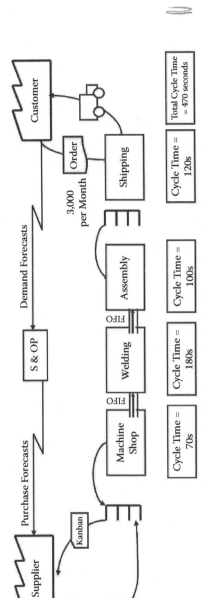

1. 470 seconds (cycle time)/600 seconds (takt time) = 78%
   This means the value stream can flow this level of demand.

2. What happens if demand increases to 60 units per day (or a takt time of 400)?
   470/400 = 118% which means this value stream cannot flow at this level of demand
   unless more resources are used to reduce cycle times.

FIGURE 3.5(b)
Understanding how Takt Time and cycle time affect flow.

must be eliminated from the business. Flow requires active management of the process by the people working in the process. Lean performance measures must be simple and easy to calculate, must be relevant to the value stream, and must drive root cause analysis and improvement.

Waste is eliminated over time through continuous improvement events. So the measures must tell the value stream the impact of every improvement event. If improvement events successfully eliminate waste, measures should improve.

The effectiveness of the pull system's management of variability must also be measured frequently and consistently. Lean companies need to know exactly how well processes are performing in delivering customer value every day, all the time. If variability is impeding flow, then it's up to the people to take short-term countermeasures to manage the issue.

Lean performance measurements are not about the measurements themselves, but about people identifying root causes and taking action. It's about what actions people do because of the measures, not simply reporting the measures. This is the primary reason why Lean performance measurement systems are usually not based in ERP (enterprise resource planning) systems. ERP systems cannot think or do root cause analysis. And they generally do not provide the information in a timely way for identifying process defects. The measurement system needs to be designed by the employees for the employees.

For flow to drive the annual productivity improvements of 10%–20% that are to be expected from Lean companies, Lean-focused measures are required. A Lean performance measurement system is different from traditional performance measurement systems based on standard costing.

Lean-focused measures have the following characteristics:

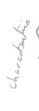

- Processes, not people, are measured.
- Measures are relevant to the process.
- Measures reveal problems and issues, which drive root-cause analysis.
- Measures are simple and easy to gather and report by the value stream.
- Measures are calculated frequently: daily or hourly at the cell and weekly in the value stream.

In general, Lean-focused measures need to measure the following characteristics of value stream performance:

- Flow
- Productivity
- Quality
- Delivery
- Cost
- Lead time

WRAP-UP

"How much money will we make from Lean?" As the Lean CFO, you will answer like this: "It depends on how fast we flow." Flow aligns with the economics of Lean because creating, maintaining, and improving flow will result in simultaneously delivering value to your customers and improving productivity.

As the Lean CFO, you must transform existing performance measurement systems away from traditional manufacturing measures to Lean performance measures that actually measure and manage flow. This will ensure that your company achieves the highest productivity gains possible. The beauty of a Lean performance measurement system is that the only way to ensure that all of the measures move in the right direction is through the use of Lean practices. This is the reason why it is necessary to eliminate all other "non-Lean" measures from the business.

Measures should drive and manage operational behavior. Aligning Lean performance measurements around flow and pull is critical to the success of a Lean Management System. In later chapters we will learn how to connect Lean performance to financial success using the Box Score. But before we talk about that, let's spend some time on the Lean office.

4

$how Me the Office Flow

INTRODUCTION

Some companies take what I call the "easy approach" to implementing Lean practices by focusing only on the manufacturing process and ignoring the rest of the company. Sometimes this occurs because a company is new to Lean and the thinking is "Lean manufacturing" not "Lean business strategy." Or the existing functional organizational structure creates cultural or political issues where people think Lean doesn't apply to them.

As I've stated a few times, the goal of 20% annual productivity improvements, company-wide, is necessary in order to achieve financial success with Lean. Your company will never get there if the entire burden for productivity improvements is on manufacturing operations. If your company ignores improving the productivity of office processes, the only way to achieve the 20% corporate goal would be for manufacturing's productivity to be much greater than 20%, which is virtually impossible to do.

As the Lean CFO, if you see that your company is defining Lean too narrowly—applying it only to the manufacturing process—then it's up to you to lead the organization in understanding how to implement Lean in administrative processes. It's important to do this early in your company's Lean journey, in order to prevent the "easy approach" to Lean from becoming part of your company's culture.

OFFICE FLOW: THE CURRENT STATE

Traditionally, there is not much focus on flow and productivity in office processes; there are a variety of reasons for this. One reason is that the focus of office work usually is on the specific technical, professional, and creative specifications related to the function, rather than on the specific needs of their customers. In accounting, the month-end numbers need to be compliant with generally accepted accounting principles (GAAP). In marketing, the latest advertisement needs to be "just right." In information technology, the infrastructure needs bandwidth and gigabytes. In new product development, the new product needs to be the most technologically advanced that can be designed and built. Yes, these are requirements, but they are internally focused on what each function's knowledge is not necessarily on the specific needs of their customers.

In manufacturing, the raw materials and products are visible and tangible. The manufacturing process work activities are physically present and can be observed. This is not always the case in office work, where much of the work is processing information on computers. It's often the opposite of manufacturing in that it is hard to "see" the actual processing and transformation of information.

The result is a high-cost, low-productivity environment: many highly paid technical specialists who work on their own, which is the perfect situation for employing Lean practices. But to understand how to employ Lean practices in the office, you need to understand the differences between manufacturing processes and office processes.

OFFICE WASTE IS MORE COMPLEX

Office waste is more complex because in addition to the seven wastes (Chapter 3) that exist in every process, office processes have more variability to deal with on a regular basis. The variability occurs in three areas: cycle times to complete work, demand, and process work flow characteristics. Not managing this variability leads to more waste. First, we will discuss this variability and then later show how to employ Lean practices in the office to eliminate or manage the variability.

Cycle Times

Cycle times to perform manufacturing activities are very predictable. There is only one way to build a particular product correctly. Standard work is created so that there is *only* one way to build a product and the cycle time is known.

Many office cycle times have inherent variability that is often unknown until the work begins. Sometimes the cause of the variability is due to the creative nature of the process, such as new product design. At other times, the cycle time varies because of the complexity of the value-added work. For example, it's a lot faster to hire a machine operator than a vice president of marketing. So it's not necessarily a bad thing that the cycle times are variable. The waste occurs when the variability is not managed and thus interrupts flow of office processes.

Demand

Like manufacturing, there is variability of demand on office processes. Manufacturing can have many customers, but they all buy a limited number of products you have designed. An office process may have multiple customers with different needs, and these needs create unique custom products and due dates. This creates variability in the rate and priority of demand.

Take accounts payable, for example. There are internal customers, such as department managers that want accurate monthly spending reports. Accounts payable also feeds expenses and balance sheet items on the monthly accrual-based financial statements for external readers. The department manager may not care about accruals, but it's necessary for financial reporting. Then there is the purchasing manager, who wants the special report of how much was paid to a supplier over the past year sorted by part number and date purchased, and he needs it in 2 hours for a meeting with the supplier and it's in the middle of the accounts payable month-end close cycle.

This variability of demand cannot be predicted. Waste is created in office processes because demand is usually pushed to the resources, who must sort and prioritize the demand on an individual basis. This creates a lot of waiting time in the process: The work is waiting to be done because the resource is working on something else.

Departmental Work Flow Characteristics

Office functions typically have more than one work flow, each of which is a distinct "production process." In accounting, the accounts payable process is distinct from the billing–accounts receivable process. Both of these processes are distinct from the month-end close process. How many process work flows are in your office function? That depends on the different types of "products" or output the department delivers to its customers.

- *Examples of continuous office processes with short cycle times:*
  - ◉ Order processing
  - Quoting
  - Engineering change requests
  - ◉ Accounts payable
  - ◉ Billing and accounts receivable
  - ◉ Responding to customer inquiries
  - IT help desk responses
  - Sales calls
- *Examples of periodic office processes with long cycle times:*
  - New product development
  - Marketing campaigns
  - Hiring new employees
  - ◉ Month-end close
  - ◉ Budgeting
  - Capital purchase and installation process
  - New customer development

The workflows that exist in a department may also have different characteristics that must be considered when trying to create flow. A workflow can be procedural such as accounts payable, or creative such as designing a marketing campaign. Procedural workflows have a tendency to have shorter, somewhat predictable cycle times while creative workflows have longer and more variable cycle times. In any department, the mix between procedural and creative processes must be clearly understood in order to create effective pull systems.

Workflows can also be continuous such as billing customers or periodic such as month-end closing. Problems with prioritization of work in a department can occur when the periodic process begins running because its priorities may conflict with those of a continuous process. Pull system design must take into account any periodic processes in a department.

Finally, some workflows are dependent on each other like a supplier-customer relationship. Problems can occur when the supplier workflow's performance doesn't match the customer workflow requirements. For example, both accounts payable and accounts receivable feed the month-end close process and if either of these processes has performance problems, month-end close could be impacted. Pull system design must consider the rate and priority of all customer demand, even if the customer is another business process.

Wastes of Overburdening and Waiting

Most office processes work as a push system, which means the work is pushed onto the employees, who must manage all the different types of variability just described. Adding to the complexity is the fact that in some departments people may work in more than one work flow, sometimes even within a workday.

A simple example of this is during the month-end close period in accounting. Though it is month end, the accountants also have their typical daily work to do, such as the daily postings in accounts receivable (A/R) and accounts payable (A/P). This means that the combined demand on a resource (process daily A/R and A/P and get month-end activities completed) may be totally different from the demand on the process (close month-end quickly.) The person is now overburdened with work, all of which has different priorities and cycle times.

In a traditional operating environment, this is known as multitasking. Office employees who can "juggle" many responsibilities at once are considered top performers. Office people who stay as late as necessary to "get the work done" are heroes. But this is really waste.

Waste of Interruptions

The final form of waste that occurs in an office but not in manufacturing is broadly defined as interruptions. These dreaded interruptions take many forms, such as phone calls that must be answered, e-mails to respond to (by the way, e-mail is one big push system), co-workers and managers stopping by to ask you a question and meetings. Most interruptions are not creating any value and all of them interrupt the actual value-added work being done by office workers.

THE FUTURE STATE: LEAN OFFICE FLOW

The challenge of creating flow in the office is to understand the difference between waste and variability. Waste can largely be eliminated through

> • *Office waste examples:*
>   • Defects—missing or incorrect information, data entry errors
>   • Overproduction—unnecessary information or reports produced (e.g., "just-in case" information)
>   • Inventory—any form of batch processing
>   • Overprocessing—excessive reviews, checking someone else's work
>   • Waiting—idle time
>   • Human motion—walking and "safaris" to find missing information
>   • Transportation—hand-offs of information between people and systems

process mapping and continuous improvement activities. Variability, on the other hand, must be managed continuously just like it is done in manufacturing. Let's look at how Lean office flow is created by designing the process, planning the work, and controlling the work.

The purpose of creating Lean office flow is to redesign office processes so they are both customer focused (delivering the value that customers want) and productive. These are the same goals as those of manufacturing. What makes this harder to do in the office is that there must be more Lean practices in place to manage the variability because it is more complex than in manufacturing.

STEP 1: DESIGN THE PROCESSES

The goal of this step is to determine exactly how many distinct processes exist in an administrative function and how they work. (Note: At this point we are not concerned with who works in which process; we just want to define the distinct flows.)

This is accomplished by looking at your function through the eyes of your customers. Define your customers and their needs. Determine what output (your "products") meets those needs. Then define exactly how many distinct work flows exist in the department to create the required output.

The Lean practice to use to do this is known as the SIPOC chart (Figure 4.1). SIPOC stands for Suppliers, Inputs, Processes, Outputs, and

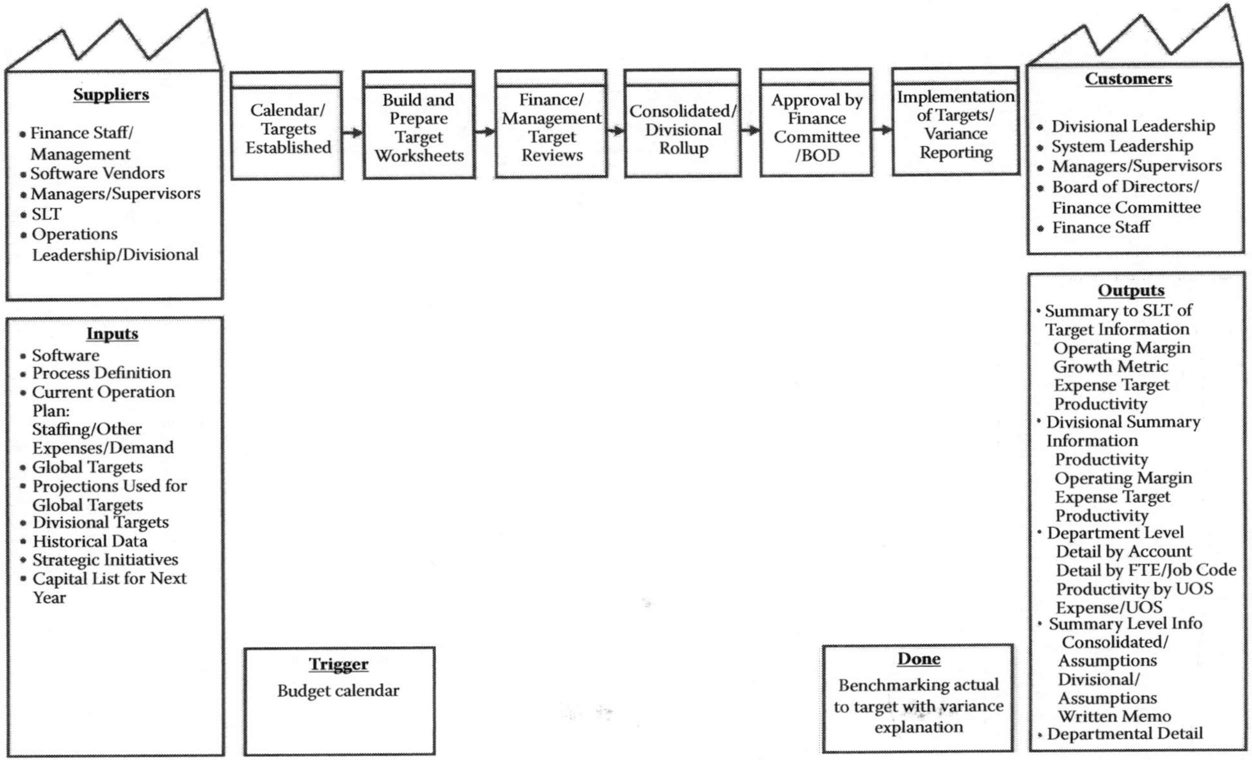

Suppliers
- Finance Staff/ Management
- Software Vendors
- Managers/Supervisors
- SLT
- Operations Leadership/Divisional

Inputs
- Software
- Process Definition
- Current Operation Plan:
- Staffing/Other Expenses/Demand
- Projections Used for Global Targets
- Global Targets
- Divisional Targets
- Historical Data
- Strategic Initiatives
- Capital List for Next Year

Calendar/ Targets Established

Build and Prepare Target Worksheets

Finance/ Management Target Reviews

Consolidated/ Divisional Rollup

Approval by Finance Committee /BOD

Implementation of Targets/ Variance Reporting

Customers
- Divisional Leadership
- System Leadership
- Managers/Supervisors
- Board of Directors/
- Finance Committee
- Finance Staff

Outputs
- Summary to SLT of Target Information Operating Margin Growth Metric Expense Target Productivity
- Divisional Summary Information Productivity Operating Margin Expense Target Productivity
- Department Level Detail by Account Detail by FTE/Job Code Productivity by UOS Expense/UOS
- Summary Level Info Consolidated/ Assumptions Divisional/ Assumptions Written Memo
- Departmental Detail

Trigger
Budget calendar

Done
Benchmarking actual to target with variance explanation

FIGURE 4.1
SIPOC chart for financial accounting.

Customers. It's a standard Lean tool used by a team to give everyone a high-level overview of all the processes. By doing this at the department level, the number of distinct processes will become apparent to all.

The next step is to understand the demand. Determine the demand patterns for products by the frequency of demand (daily, hourly, weekly) and the variability of demand. The Lean practice to employ to do this is calculating takt time, which was explained in Chapter 3 and illustrated in Figure 3.5.

The final step in the design phase is to map the processes, using standard Lean value stream mapping tools. Map the value-added process steps: the minimum work that must be completed to deliver the output. These steps must be mapped in the proper sequence required to create and deliver the output.

STEP 2: PLAN THE WORK

I guess a better description for this section would be "A Plan to Manage the Variability." What is important to understand when planning the work is that the Flow Time of work through any process is determined by the queue of work in the process. This means the larger the queue of work in the process is, the longer is the flow time. Pushing all of the variability into the process increases the queue of work because the resources must not only do the work but also manage all the variability. By creating a plan to prioritize the demand and creating single piece flow, the queue of work will be limited in the process and flow time will be decreased.

Prioritizing Demand

Standardized work needs to be created to prioritize demand based on the frequency in which it changes. This prioritization needs to be done *before the work is released* into the process. Think of this as a triage process. Based on the calculation of Takt Time, how often prioritization needs to occur should become apparent. Here are some examples.

In procedural processes with short cycle times and predictable demand, such as processing supplier invoices in accounts payable, daily prioritization by the accounts payable team is probably possible. In a process with short cycle times and unpredictable demand, such as order processing, the prioritization would need to be more active. This can be accomplished by dedicating a person to managing the prioritization actively so that the people processing the orders can simply "pull" the next highest priority order.

Single Piece Flow

The objective here is to create a pull system in an office process. In manufacturing, this is done by working on one unit at a time, or working in the smallest batches possible. The pull system limits the work to the unit or small batch per process step.

The first step to creating an office pull system is to define a unit of work. Think of a unit as a cadence, or standard cycle time, for the process. The objective is to make the unit as short a time frame as possible based on how the process works. This means that a process with a short cycle time, such as order processing, may define a unit as 30 minutes of work. A process that has a longer cycle time, such as new product design, may define a unit of work as 1 week of work.

The purpose of defining the standard unit of work is used to recognize the inherent variability in cycle time to complete different types of work so that the work can be limited in the process. Continuing the order-processing example, a simple order may be one unit (30 minutes) of work, whereas a complex order may be two units of work (60 minutes). These are time estimates and the actual cycle time to complete a particular unit may be different depending on the actual work involved.

The work is limited in the process by releasing it in the smallest possible batch sizes. One batch must be completed before moving on to the other batch. Customer service may define a batch as 1 hour of work. This means that each customer service representative will be assigned either two simple orders, or one complex order, to complete before being assigned the next batch. The idea is to work on one batch at a time, from start to completion, before pulling the next batch.

STEP 3: CONTROLLING THE WORK

Controlling the work is about executing flow on a daily basis. In manufacturing, the combination of visual signals and Lean practices regulates the work throughout the value stream to create flow. Here is how it is done in the office.

> **"WE HAVE STANDARD WORK!"**
>
> People think that their existing office processes have standard work, but what they really have is detailed procedural manuals, most of which sit idly in desks or on bookshelves.
>
> Standard work is the proven way to perform an activity in the desired sequence of steps, the time required to perform the step, and other elements that ensure the quality of the work. Standard work is simple, visual, and self-correcting.

Level Scheduling to 80% of Capacity

All of the possible types of office variability cannot be predicted therefore they cannot be scheduled; always leave some buffer capacity for the unexpected. Schedule to 80% of capacity, whether it be for the entire process or its team members. Office workers have 8 hours of capacity per day, so only schedule 6 hours per day.

Balance the work each day (or whatever the cadence) by leveling the schedule among the workers available. This is accomplished through a visual scheduling board, where the team determines its work priorities for the day and assigns tasks to each worker. Tasks can be rotated at regular intervals to balance out the type of work activities performed. The daily schedule is the value-added work that must flow that day.

Control Interruptions

Build standard work to control the interruptions. Build time into the schedule (such as the buffer capacity) to deal with interruptions and not interrupt flow. Or create an "Interruption Meister," one person designated to handle all interruptions for a certain time period. This will free the other resources to flow the work. Finally, if people are not available because they must attend meetings or are out of the office, they cannot be scheduled for any work.

Andon

Build standard work to "stop and fix" problems with flow as they arise. Visual signals need to be in place to signal to the process that there are problems with flow, which lead to stopping the work either to fix the problem or to employ a short-term countermeasure to resume flow.

Visual Workplace

Finally, visualize the management of work with a flow board and team meetings. The flow board and meetings should be set up based on the cadence of the process. Daily boards are best, but weekly boards may be better in functions where the cycle times are long. However, if the department has a mixture of processes with short and long cycle times, go with daily boards. The work schedule should be visible and organized according to the priority of demand. Longer term planning—looking out a week or month ahead at expected demand—should also be visible. Office process teams will use the visual boards and daily performance measures to monitor and manage the variability to create office flow. Figure 4.2 illustrates how an office process is controlled with flow boards, team meetings, and daily scheduling.

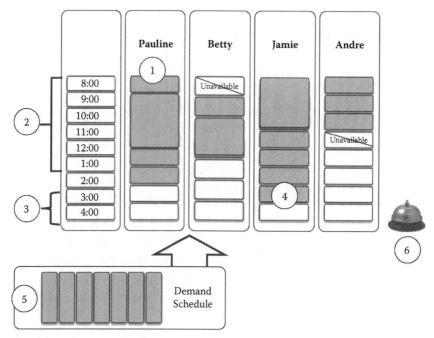

Legend
1. All value-added work is converted into "units," based on the estimated cycle time to complete the work (meaning from start to finish, uninterrupted).
2. Team members prioritize their value-added work each day. This becomes the sequence by which the work will be pulled by each team member.
3. Buffer capacity is left in daily schedule for (1) longer than planned cycle time; (2) unplanned customer demand; and (3) non-value-added but necessary work (phone calls, e-mails, etc.).
4. Daily balancing of work – during the daily morning meeting, team reviews the schedule and determines how to balance the work so all priority work for the day flows. In this case, Jamie doesn't have enough capacity to complete his priority work but Andre does. Andre picks up some of Jamie's tasks so all work flows for the day.
5. Team member standard work: If work is completed faster than planned, team member pulls the next highest priority demand from the demand schedule.
6. Team member standard work: If a team member falls behind (due to longer than planned cycle times), he signals team members or flow manager to reassign work to free resource.

FIGURE 4.2
Daily schedule board.

WRAP-UP: OFFICE FLOW AND THE LEAN CFO

"We're not a factory" is often the response heard from administrative people when it comes to applying Lean practices in administrative processes. I think this response occurs for two reasons. First, office people deep down understand all the variability they face that doesn't exist in the factory. Second, they think Lean is only about eliminating waste rather than creating flow. The Lean CFO can do two things: Explain the financial benefits of office flow and create flow in accounting processes to illustrate how it works.

Administrative department performance is traditionally measured against a budget. And usually the largest single expense in administrative departments is people. So the traditional solution is to control head count to control the budget. As the Lean CFO, you can shift emphasis from head count to productivity through the implementation of Lean performance measures, which will be discussed next in Chapter 5.

Implementing office flow will dramatically reduce the rate of selling and general and administrative spending over time. As office processes generate annual productivity improvements, your company will not have to increase office head count and may be able to reduce it by not replacing people when they leave the company. That is real productivity.

Finally, create an office flow laboratory in accounting processes. Flow is a difficult concept to grasp if you have never actually experienced it. Most employees in a company participate in company accounting processes as suppliers, customers, and sometimes both in the same process. Eliminating waste and creating flow in these processes impacts everyone— not just accounting workers. Demonstrate what daily office flow looks like to begin the journey of driving annual 20% productivity improvements.

5

Measure Lean Performance, Not Profits

INTRODUCTION

One of your primary responsibilities as CFO is to be able to link operating performance to financial results so that you can explain the financial statements to their readers. In a traditional manufacturing company with a lot of inventory, the impact of inventory on the financial results often obscures the impact of operational performance. This leads to the creation of traditional performance measurements that typically focus on three areas of operational performance: financial, performance to plan, and key performance indicators.

TRADITIONAL MEASUREMENTS

Financially based measurements (any number with a dollar sign in front of it) are automatically backward looking. Sure, the root cause can be identified, but nothing can be done to change the outcome. The financial performance of a factory is typically based on measuring actual to budget. The process is simple: Create a monthly expense budget, measure actual expenses against that budget, and explain the differences. This leads to the thinking that factories are cost centers and that their job is to try to reduce costs as much as possible.

Performance to plan is based on overhead absorption and variance analysis. Standards of operating performance are set up in the production reporting system and are included in bills of material, routers, labor rates, and overhead rates. Reporting actual production and usage of resources against these standards generates the variances. Here, the goal of the factory is to absorb as much overhead as possible while maintaining favorable

In an organization with value streams but organized by functional departments, people tend naturally to "look up" toward the functional departments. Remove old functional department measures and make value stream measures the only measures on which people must focus.

variances. The only way to accomplish this is to employ traditional manufacturing practices.

The final set of measures is key performance indicators, or KPIs, which have become increasingly popular because people realize absorption and variance numbers don't really tell the "whole picture" of a traditional manufacturing operation. Most KPIs are based on the vertical organizational structure and focus on supply chain performance, more operational performance measures, and delivery and logistic measures. The goal of these KPIs is to maximize each function's performance. So on top of financial and operating performance, a plant has to contend with measures from quality, supply chain, operations, human resources, and maybe a few others.

The result is too many measures that people don't really understand. If you have a lot of measures in your plants (and many companies have upwards of 50–100 measures per plant), all this does is force operations to make trade-offs in performance. Operations must decide which performance measures it will try to improve because it doesn't know how, or can't, improve all of them at the same time.

And you, as the CFO, and your finance staff continually try to fit these pieces of the puzzle together. Some months the pieces fit very well—profits up, shipments up, inventory down, absorption up, KPIs good—and you have an easy month explaining the results. In other months, there seems to be no connection: profits down, shipments up, inventory up, absorption not so good, and KPIs mixed. These are the months you hate having to present the financial reports, as everyone is looking to you for the reasons, and there is no connection between performance and financial results.

LEAN MEASUREMENTS

Lean companies also recognize that optimization of the entire value stream flow is the primary goal. And this goal must take precedence against all departmental goals. When it comes to operating performance, Lean companies employ a different philosophy: Understand the present to change the future. This forms the basis for making improvements. Changing the future will require specific actions and changes to operating performance.

As your company's Lean CFO, you must recognize early in the Lean journey that performance measurements must change to become aligned with Lean operating practices. The two operating goals of any value stream are to deliver value and to improve productivity continuously. It's up to you to establish the link between the economics of Lean and your company's performance measurement system.

Existing performance measurements that are not Lean focused must be eliminated from the business; otherwise, conflict will occur. Performance measures that are based solely on the vertical structure of the company must be eliminated or modified. The modification of these measures requires that the department, such as quality or supply chain, have measures on the department that focus on its ability to support the value stream. In a traditional company, the department dictates performance to operations; in a Lean company, the value stream dictates performance to the department.

You make this happen by changing the measures, linking the measures to the Lean strategy and practices, and using the measures properly to drive problem solving.

CHANGING THE MEASURES

In Chapter 3 we learned that creating flow in value streams is a critical first step to unlocking the financial potential of Lean. An outcome of flow is productivity improvements. But creating flow is not the end game: It must continuously be improved through kaizen events and smaller continuous improvement projects.

The key to achieving flow and improvements is to measure the correct aspects of value stream performance (Figure 5.1). If the Lean-focused measures are used, the only way to improve the measures is to practice Lean all the time. Here are the five aspects of process performance that need to be measured:

Flow: Because creating flow in a value stream will reduce and then limit the inventory present in the value stream, the best measure of flow is

> Don't be too concerned about detailed measuring of the value of your inventory; be concerned about reducing the days of inventory.

related to inventory velocity: turns, days, or dock-to-dock time. Creating flow will allow orders to move faster through the value stream and drive revenue growth. Improving flow creates more capacity to meet additional demand without increasing costs.

Quality: Poor quality interrupts flow, causing later deliveries, lowering customer satisfaction, and negatively impacting productivity. Who does the quality work and when are also factors that impact operational performance. An important part of Lean practices is building perfection into processes. This is the reason for "quality at the source," where operators building the product do the inspection of their work immediately, or quality people are assigned to value streams and their work is incorporated into the flow.

If quality at the source is standard work in the value stream, then defects will be discovered quickly, root causes will be easier to identify, and continuous improvement will ultimately reduce defect rates and reduce materials spending.

The reduction of defects will improve productivity because the time that was being used to create defects is now being used to create good product. Labor and machine spending per product will be reduced. Improving quality also improves customer satisfaction by improving such things as on-time deliveries and reducing returns and warranty costs.

Delivery: Delivering on time to the customer request date has the potential to set your company apart from the competition by providing value to the market. Many companies use customer service or sales functions to negotiate with customers' delivery dates or promise dates. Then they measure on-time delivery against the promise date. And guess what? The ratio of on time to promise date is always very high, which wrongly tells the company that it is performing well, and that there is no need for improvement. The whole process of negotiating delivery dates is waste.

Measure on-time delivery against customer request date—period. Meet your customer needs in terms of delivery and you will create value, which will drive growth in demand and revenue. And if you can be the first company in your industry to do this, you will set yourself apart from the competition.

	Measurement description	What does it measure?	Lean practices required
Monthly Lean company strategic measures	Sales per person	Productivity of business	Create flow in all business processes
	On-time shipments	Ability of value streams to deliver customer value	Eliminate waste from order receipt to delivery
	Inventory days	Rate of material flow	Create material flow from supplier through operations to customer
	Sales growth	Delivering value to customers	Focus organization on value-added activities
	Cash flow	Delivery of value and improving productivity	Eliminate waste and create flow throughout the business
	Average lead time	Flow	Effectiveness of pull systems
Weekly Lean value stream measures	Sales per person	Productivity of value stream	Flow demand and eliminate waste
	On-time shipments	Percentage of shipments delivered by customer request date	Pull system execution
	Inventory days	Material flow	Pull system from suppliers through operations
	First time through	Quality	Operator-led quality and standard work
	Average cost per unit	Productivity	Flow demand and eliminate waste
Daily or hourly Lean cell measures	Day by the hour	Schedule attainment to takt time	Short-term countermeasures to maintain flow
	First time through	Defects	Operator-led quality-eliminating defects
	WIP to SWIP	Pull system execution	Identify obstacles to flow and take corrective action

FIGURE 5.1

Lean performance measures.

On-time delivery is an excellent measurement because paying attention to the reasons why you ship late reveals a lot of valuable information about how to improve value stream flow.

Lead time: Lead time is the total time it takes demand to flow through a process. In operations, lead time starts at receipt of a customer order and ends with delivery of the product to the customer. From a Lean viewpoint, lead time is the sum of total cycle time and waste time. Total cycle time is the value-added time it takes to make a product. Lead time is an excellent performance measure because it requires looking at how the value stream performs as a system, rather than just looking at the individual process steps of the value stream.

Reducing lead time requires elimination of the waste time, which is accomplished by establishing flow and using a continuous improvement system (described in Chapter 3). Trying to eliminate waste using any other method simply won't work.

Short lead times create value for customers. If customers know your lead times are short, they can reduce their inventory levels and free up cash. Additionally, they can reduce their delivery times to their customers. If you have the shortest lead times in the market, you will gain a competitive advantage. Demand and revenue will increase.

Productivity: The definition of productivity is output divided by input. Lean companies define input as resources. Output is simply shipments to customer. If Lean practices are in place and delivering value to customers every day, then demand will be increasing. If Lean practices are eliminating waste, then you will be able to meet this demand with your existing resources, or at least add resources at a much lower rate than in the past. Your company will rapidly move to unprecedented levels of profits and cash.

Now here is the tricky part for the Lean CFO. You have to stop the company from using all other performance measures. If you want to drive substantial Lean improvement in your value streams, then you need to

The objective of a Lean performance measurement system is to improve productivity, lead time, delivery, flow, and cost simultaneously. The only way to accomplish this is through Lean practices. This is the reason why all other operational performance measures must be eliminated.

limit the measurements to the critical few that focus the value stream on its Lean objectives. If value streams focus on these five aspects of performance, the only way to improve every measure is to be Lean. Using any other measures at the value stream level will take away from this effort to improve continuously. The economics of Lean are simple, so measuring performance to achieve financial success should also be as simple.

LINK MEASURES TO LEAN STRATEGY

All Lean performance measures must be linked to the Lean business strategy; they must be relevant and understandable to the area being measured; and they must be actionable. The primary purpose of Lean performance measures is to expose the problems of poor performance within your company's value streams, identify the root causes, and take corrective action. The corrective action may be a short-term countermeasure, a continuous improvement event, or a larger breakthrough change.

The best way to ensure that all measures line up with the overall company strategy is to design the Lean-focused measurements using a performance measurement linkage chart. A linkage chart is built by a cross-functional exercise including senior management, Lean leadership, operations, and other key managers.

Linkage charts can be created for every value stream and also every administrative process. Figure 5.2 (two parts) is a sample linkage chart for a value stream. Figure 5.3 is a sample linkage chart for sales and marketing and Figure 5.4 is a sample linkage chart for new product development.

Management begins the linkage chart development by identifying the strategic objectives of the business and creating monthly company performance measures. The purpose of the corporate measures is to tell the management of the company whether or not the Lean Business strategy is working.

After company measures have been determined, the value streams will set goals for the improvements that are required for achievement of the corporate measures. Value stream measurements are then created, showing the value stream's progress toward achieving these changes and improvements.

Continued

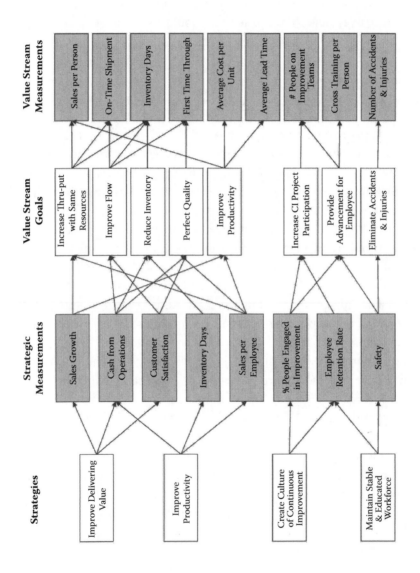

FIGURE 5.2

Linkage chart for an order fulfillment value stream.

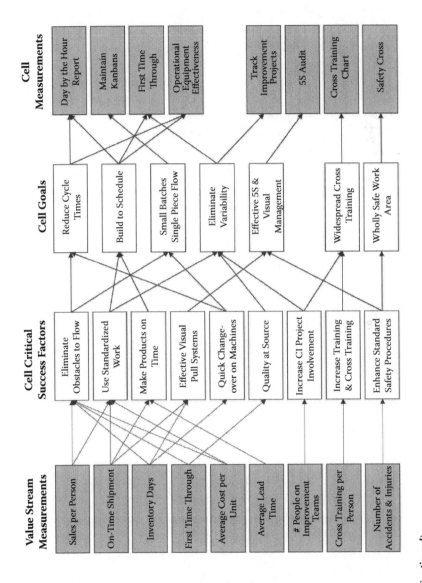

FIGURE 5.2 (Continued)
Linkage chart for an order fulfillment value stream.

> Senior management has two functions in a Lean performance measurement system: Set annual improvement targets based on strategy and help value streams solve problems when they come to management for help. value stream and cell measures are not reported up to senior management. They need to visit value stream and cell meetings if they want to know what is going on.

Finally, each work cell will do the same thing, namely: develop daily and/or hourly measures that are linked to the actions required by each cell in order for the value stream to fulfill its goals.

The cross-functional approach to developing a linkage chart makes measures relevant and simple because the people who will be using the measures have a say in developing their measures. Compare this to the traditional approach to creating performance measures, where management determines the measures, finance distributes them, and operations is required to explain measures that they don't understand.

Lean performance measures need to be simple for two reasons. First, these measures will be reported more frequently—hourly, daily, or weekly—so they cannot take a long time to calculate. Second, simple measures will focus the teams on identifying the root causes of poor performance, which is the key to driving productivity improvements.

USING LEAN PERFORMANCE MEASUREMENTS

At one level, creating the measures is the easy part; the application and use of the measures is often more difficult because it requires changing the style of management of the company, as well as each individual manager. Fortunately, there are standard Lean practices that can be employed. If they are employed, performance measures will improve. If they are not employed, you will probably not see the overall improvement of productivity that you want.

The first practice is Visual Management of all performance measures (Figure 5.5). Every cell, value stream, and company measure is clearly displayed on a performance board. There are no secrets in a Lean company!

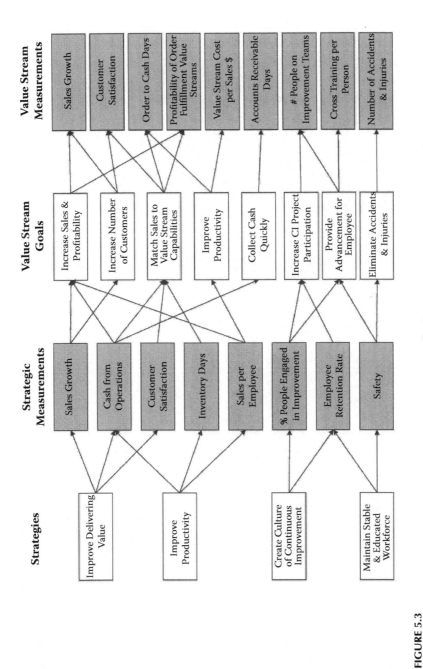

FIGURE 5.3

Example of linkage chart for an administrative process: Sales/Marketing value stream measurements.

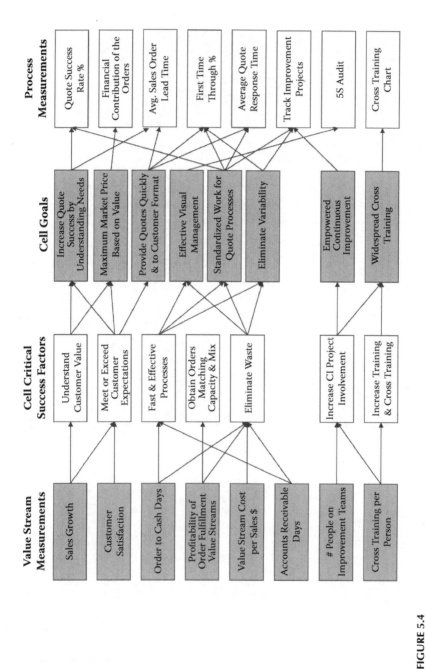

FIGURE 5.4

Linkage chart for a sales/marketing value stream quote process.

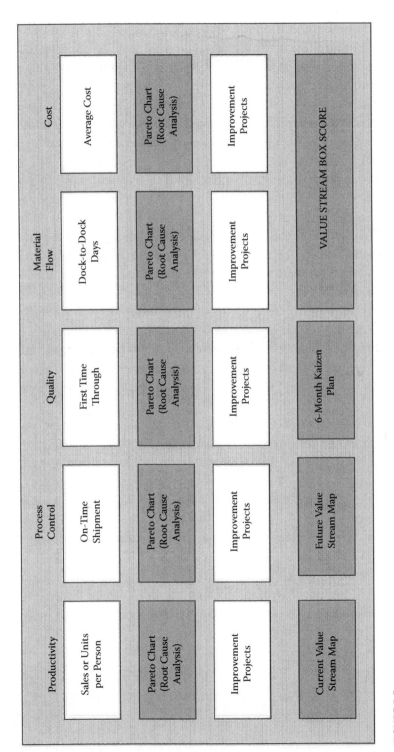

FIGURE 5.5
Value Stream continuous improvement board schematic.

Think of a performance board as a storyboard. It tells the actual performance of the area in such a simple format that anyone can come up to the board and read it without asking questions or waiting for a presentation.

The key to effective performance boards is "less is more." Here is what is needed on a performance board: measurement trend against the goal, a Pareto chart of the major root causes of why the measures are not meeting goals, the status of each improvement activity undertaken to remove root causes, and a list of major kaizen events.

Next, the measures and performance boards are used in the cycle of daily, weekly, and monthly meetings to review operating performance. Cells conduct daily meetings to answer the question: "Are we meeting customer requirements today?" Value stream teams meet weekly to answer the question: "Are we improving toward the future state?" And finally, management meets monthly to answer the question: "Is the Lean business strategy working?"

The purpose of these meetings is to identify the root causes of the problems and identify the necessary improvements. Ideally, the cell or value stream can quickly identify the improvement; but sometimes the necessary improvement requires skills, expertise, or experience beyond the scope of the value stream or cell. This is where manager standard work comes into play.

Manager standard work (Figure 5.6) is the daily and weekly routine to which all managers must adhere as part of their position. Manager standard work is not optional. Manager standard work takes priority over all other meetings. Manager standard work consists of attending cell and value stream meetings, doing gemba walks, and solving problems. Cells and value streams need to elevate root causes they cannot solve to the proper level of management so that the proper resources can be assigned to solving the problem.

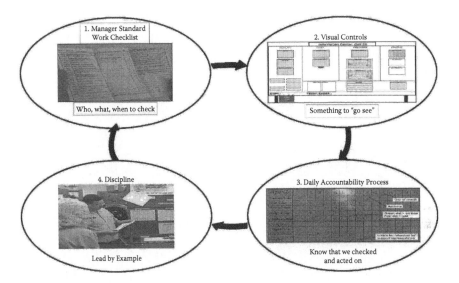

FIGURE 5.6
Management standard work.

WRAP-UP

The combination of Lean performance measures, performance boards, and manager standard work creates the Lean performance measurement system, which will lead to focusing value streams on its two objectives: delivering value and driving productivity improvements. Being able to measure these aspects of Lean performance will establish a clear link for you between operating results and financial performance.

As the Lean CFO, you must ensure the integrity of the entire performance measurement system. The "right" measures for your company are the set of measures that require Lean practices, tools, and methods to drive productivity, flow, quality, delivery, and lead time improvements simultaneously. Some current measures might work, but it's more likely that the company will have to create some new measures and stop using many existing ones. The "right" measures drive root cause analysis and solve operational problems; they don't just skim surface issues.

Getting the right measures in place early in your Lean journey and ending the use of all non-Lean measures ensure that Lean practices will become established, allowing you to move on to the next area of change: managing costs.

6

It's about Spending, Not Costs

INTRODUCTION

Your primary job as CFO is financial review and analysis. You have to explain your company's financial results to all readers of your financial statements. You also want to understand your company's costs and trends, plus you want to identify opportunities. Is there a company out there that wouldn't like to reduce costs?

Cost analysis for external financial reporting must align with your financial statements, SEC reporting (if applicable), and industry standards. Your company probably has well-established practices for external financial analysis. This chapter is going to address the way a Lean company analyzes its costs internally by management to drive financial performance.

TRADITIONAL COST MANAGEMENT

You typically employ a variety of tools to establish links between operational performance and financial results. Annual budgets are set and actual results are compared to the budget. Some companies create a financial forecast (which is essentially an updated budget) and do actual-to-forecast analyses. Manufacturing companies employ production-reporting systems to track and explain operational performance to plan. Finally, product-costing systems, such as standard costing and activity-based costing, are used to explain the impact of inventory on the financial statements.

These systems all share common characteristics: They are based on analyzing historical costs; they are complex and time consuming, and they rely on actual-to-plan analysis.

The analysis of any cost is historical. You are looking backward to understand why a cost occurred. Sure, you can find out the reason the cost was incurred, but all you can do is explain it. The cost cannot be changed.

Think about how much time and effort go into your annual budgeting process. Yet, in the end, many people remain skeptical about the budget. Think about how much time goes into the monthly analysis to explain the actual-to-budget numbers. If you have a standard costing system, think about how much time goes into setting standards and then into comparing actual to standards. And in the end, how many people truly believe these systems are very effective and do what they are intended to do?

Nonfinancial people have a difficult time understanding generally accepted accounting principles (GAAP)-based financial statements. They don't understand the accruals, reserve adjustments, and inventory valuation work that must be done to create GAAP-compliant statements. Complex financial statements create confusion for non-financial people.

Finally, people dislike the annual budgeting process (or the annual standard setting process) because of all the assumptions they have to make about the future. As your company creates a monthly detailed expense budget by department, in essence what you are asking your managers to do is predict the future. No one can accurately predict what business conditions will be like months in advance. If they could, then they could probably make a lot of money doing that for a living.

VALUE STREAM ACCOUNTING

As the Lean CFO, you need to transition your company away from traditional types of cost management and create a Lean cost management system based on value stream accounting. This is necessary because continuing to use traditional cost management systems in a Lean company will create conflict. Traditional cost management systems lead to traditional manufacturing solutions, which conflict with Lean.

"It's about spending, not costs." This is the message you send as the Lean CFO. Don't be concerned with trying to calculate the cost of anything—a product, customer, process, product line, etc. It's all worthless information because costs have to be allocated, and the basis of allocation has nothing to do with the root cause of the cost. To control and reduce spending, you must understand the root causes of the spending, which lie in operational practices and behavior of your value streams.

Spending money involves making a business decision or taking some specific action. If decisions or actions can be changed, then spending will be changed. If spending can be changed, costs will ultimately change. This is the same basis as that of the Lean performance measurement system: Create simple, relevant measures that reinforce Lean practices and identify deviations from them. Use improvement events to remove root causes and improve performance.

VALUE STREAM COSTING

The first component of value stream accounting is value stream costing, which assigns actual, direct costs to value streams. All costs are assigned where the spending occurs. This means that costs that are traditionally allocated under a product costing system are no longer allocated. This is done so that Lean problem-solving methodologies can be effectively employed.

Lean problem solving is dependent on identifying the root causes because, once a root cause can be understood, it can be changed, eliminated, or managed. This is how continuous improvement works in Lean manufacturing operations. From a cost perspective, the root cause of the cost is some kind of decision or action. By assigning actual costs where the spending decision occurs and not allocating it any further, we can employ everyone in the company in root cause analysis of spending. And by increasing the frequency in which costs are reported—from monthly to weekly—it becomes easier to identify root causes and change or reduce spending. Let's look at some examples of how it becomes much easier to manage spending with value stream costing.

Material Spending

In financial accounting, material costs are components of inventories on your balance sheet and cost of goods sold on the income statement. In value stream costing, these are expenses when incurred. Right now you might be thinking: "But that is not GAAP!" Read on and remember what

THE MATERIAL COST REDUCTION TRAP

If your only focus is the lowest possible material price, you will probably get it by trading off on inventory, quality, delivery, and/or lead time, which will negatively impact flow and productivity.

we are trying to do: reduce spending on materials. Material spending needs to be analyzed by its components: price and quantity.

In traditional product cost systems, all that matters is the lowest material price. This leads to non-Lean behavior such as buying excess material in order to secure the largest purchase price discount. Lean companies recognize that price is just one component of the entire supplier relationship, which also includes lead time, delivery, and quality. All four components must be considered in terms of the specific performance required of suppliers to maintain and improve material flow within your value streams. Lean companies understand that the price they pay for materials is based on the value received from the supplier. In general, unless you can dictate all terms to your suppliers, it's best to concentrate on developing excellent relationships with suppliers based on the value you require from them.

Reducing material quantity on hand is where a difference can be made in material spending (Figure 6.1). By reporting actual material spending on a weekly value stream income statement, value streams will be driven to reduce material spending by purchasing materials only when needed and flowing materials faster. In a Pull System, the quantity of material on hand is limited to actual demand plus some buffer stock.

Reducing scrap and rework will also reduce material spending. For this to occur, we need to measure quality incidents at every production cell daily and in every value stream weekly. Measures such as "First Time Through" or "First Pass Yield" will give us the true root causes of quality from which corrective action can be taken, as was discussed in detail in Chapter 5.

The final method of reducing material spending is in product design. Redesigning products with less material or substituting less expensive materials is an option, but it must be considered in terms of customer value, not simply material cost.

These same principles apply to managing the spending of all other material costs of a company, such as manufacturing supplies, spare parts, and office supplies.

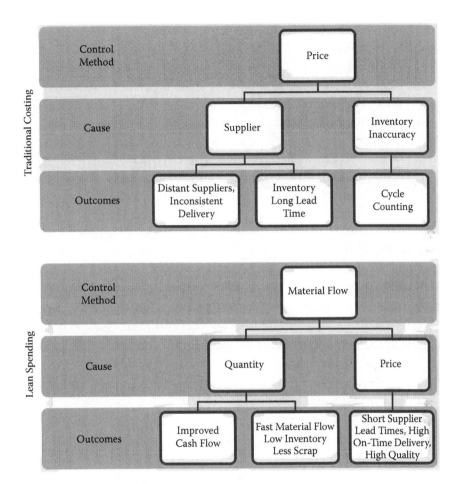

FIGURE 6.1
Managing material expense.

Labor Spending

The traditional approach to managing labor costs is quite simple: Try to keep reducing it. From a total labor cost perspective, it's all about measuring head count and overtime hours. From a product cost perspective, it's all about reducing the direct labor content of product costs and making sure that it is as efficient as possible. These approaches are not very effective because they don't address the real root causes of how much a company spends on labor.

Lean companies do not view labor as just an operating expense. They have a different view: Labor is a resource. Labor provides the capacity to create the value that your customers want from you. There are two primary

> **Myth: head count is important.**
> Fact: the ability to maintain productivity levels, regardless of the rate of demand, and improve productivity by 10%–20% annually is important.
> **Myth: overtime needs to be analyzed and explained.**
> Fact: if you feel like you have an overtime problem, you really have a capacity problem. Understand the root causes of nonproductive capacity and eliminate them and see overtime go down.

root causes of your labor cost: the total amount of labor required and the productivity of that labor.

Labor spending is based on the total amount of labor is the total number of people that are assigned to your value streams. Lean companies recognize that departmental barriers, especially those between frontline operations and traditional manufacturing support functions (such as quality, maintenance, and engineering) are barriers to improving flow. This is why Lean companies assign as many people as possible to work in value streams fulltime. Value stream costing recognizes this as labor expense on the value stream income statement.

Lean companies understand that labor spending really boils down to the productivity of the labor (Figure 6.2). They are not as concerned with the total amount of labor, as long as productivity continues to increase. This is the reason why Lean companies simply charge the actual cost of labor to value streams. They want value stream managers to focus more on measuring and improving productivity.

Productivity is the ratio of output to input of the entire value stream. Lean companies define output as demand or shipments, not production. Input is the total labor, such as hours worked. If productivity is improving, then output (shipments) is increasing at a greater rate than input (hours worked). This means that the rate of spending on labor is increasing at a lower rate than the rate of revenue growth, which means profits are increasing.

What should matter is consistently improving productivity 20% annually. People are unproductive for one reason: The processes they work in, which have been designed by the company, are not Lean. Low productivity is generally not the workers' fault; it is caused by poor processes. Using traditional measurements like labor efficiency or head count sends the message that poor productivity is their fault. Productivity will only

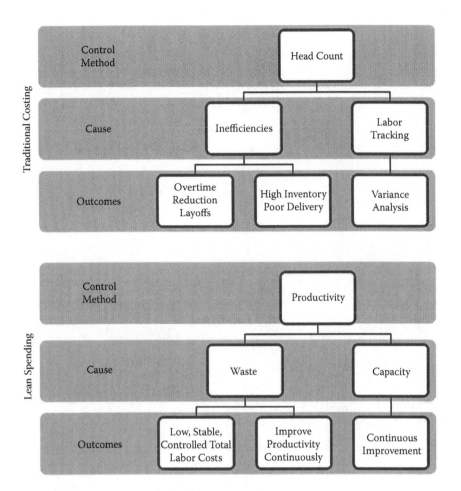

FIGURE 6.2
Managing labor expense.

increase when the waste is eliminated from the value stream, allowing workers to focus on delivering value.

In an environment of increasing productivity, adding more people means that demand is increasing. As long as productivity rates are maintained when people are hired, it doesn't matter how large your head count is. You will be making money.

Machine Spending

The traditional approach to managing machine costs focuses on maximizing the utilization. This means long production runs with few changeovers, typically resulting in large batch sizes and too much inventory.

Machines are just like labor: They are your capacity, and the focus should be on improving productivity (Figure 6.3). To improve machine productivity, Lean companies focus on identifying the root causes of why the machine cannot run if demand is present. One area of focus is downtime. Lean companies want to minimize unplanned downtime because this disrupts flow. Total preventative maintenance (TPM) practices will minimize unplanned downtime, and because TPM is planned, flow will not be disrupted.

Other root causes of high machine spending are quality problems with the product and the rate of production of the machine. If a machine is

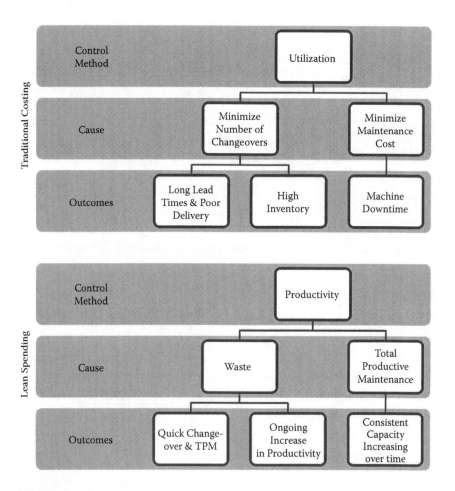

FIGURE 6.3
Managing machine expense.

producing poor quality, costs go up. Quality measures address this root cause. If the machine is producing at a lower rate than customer demand, costs go up. The combination of managing to takt time and continuous improvement addresses this root cause.

Changeover is also a primary root cause that must be addressed. To improve machine productivity, changeover must first be stabilized and standardized, and then reduced. Continuous improvement will address ongoing changeover time. If changeover cannot be avoided, then it must be managed using level scheduling techniques.

Quality Spending

Traditional companies make an attempt to calculate the "cost of quality." The most popular method to do this is to use the standard costing system: the total material cost scrapped or the total product cost scrapped (including the labor and overhead).

The primary reason for doing this is to be able to report summary information to senior management when they ask this question: How much is poor quality costing the company?

The real costs of quality from a Lean viewpoint are lost productivity, poor delivery, high material spending, and the impact of poor quality on revenue (Figure 6.4). None of this information comes from standard costing. It comes from measuring quality at the source.

We want to measure quality incidents at every production cell daily and in every value stream weekly. Measures such as first time through or first pass yield will give us the true root causes of quality, from which corrective action can be taken immediately in the cell or value stream. This will improve flow and lower quality spending. Ultimately, Lean companies attempt to eliminate quality inspection as a separate department and incorporate it directly into the value stream.

Maintenance Spending

The traditional approach to controlling maintenance costs is to establish a complex work-order system to track the time and materials spent on each maintenance job. This is good information to have, but because this is a tracking system, it does little to establish the root causes of maintenance issues.

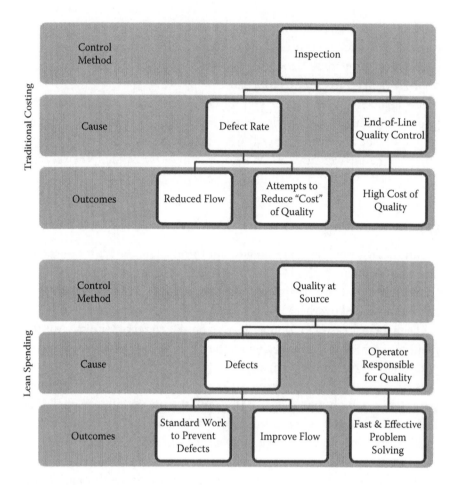

FIGURE 6.4
Managing quality expense.

The goal of Lean maintenance is to minimize downtime (Figure 6.5). One method employed to accomplish this is by creating maintenance flow, as described in Chapter 3. Additional practices employed include total preventative maintenance and maintenance at the source. The end result is the lowest cost, most productive maintenance function.

Material Management Spending

Material management exists because inventory is out of control (Figure 6.6). With the establishment of pull systems throughout production, inventory will be reduced, and inventory levels will be limited.

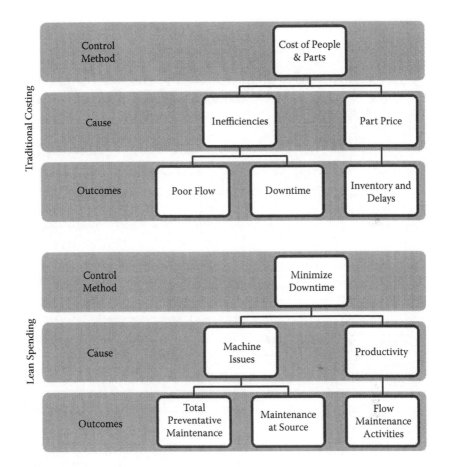

FIGURE 6.5
Managing maintenance expense.

Establishing point-of-use stocking location of raw materials and components will eliminate the need for multiple inventory locations and movement of inventory. The traditional role of material management—moving inventory and cycle counting—is made obsolete.

Receiving Inspection Spending

Receiving inspection exists because of poor supplier quality and excessive inventory. Like the material management function, the overall goal is to make the receiving inspection function obsolete. This is accomplished primarily through supplier certification, where you establish relationships with your key suppliers in terms of price, delivery, quality, and lead time.

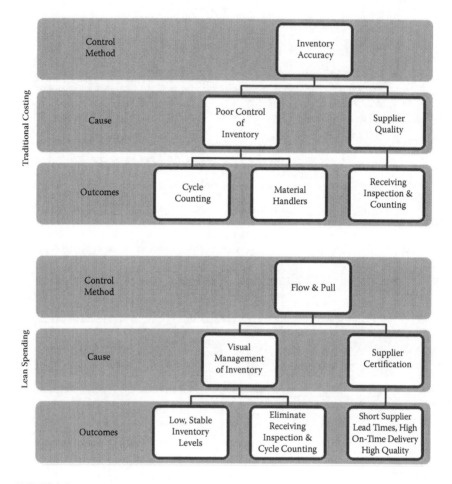

FIGURE 6.6
Managing material management expense.

Kanban is established between value streams and certified suppliers, who deliver directly to the point of use.

VALUE STREAM INCOME STATEMENT

Spending money involves making a business operating decision or taking some other type of action. If the decisions and actions can be changed, spending can be changed. This is the foundation of value stream accounting.

As Lean CFO, your first priority is to focus the efforts of the value stream on controlling spending. How much is the value stream spending period to period? And is the spending consistent and tied directly to that week's delivery of products and services to the customers? A weekly value stream income statement will do this. Total value stream expense is the amount of money a value stream is spending. The job of the value stream manager is to identify the root causes of spending and change decisions and actions. Looking at expenses on a weekly basis makes it easier to identify root causes. Report as much spending as possible on a weekly basis.

Your second priority is to begin using the combination of the value stream income statement and kaizen events to reduce spending. Eliminating waste will reduce spending. Have value streams hunt down the classic seven wastes in their value streams and eliminate them. Measure the impact of every kaizen event using the Box Score. If something is to be called a kaizen event, it must involve measurable improvement to the Box Score; otherwise, it is not a kaizen event.

Third, create a value stream income statement for your company and make it the only income statement used by management to analyze the business (Figure 6.7). Show the profitability of each value stream separately. Report all costs not assigned to value streams, such as new product development, sales, marketing, accounting, and other administrative expenses, as support. The value stream operating profit is what is generated by flowing demand and improving productivity. It will improve over time as Lean practices mature.

All items "below" the value stream profit line are financial accounting adjustments that accounting must make to create GAAP-compliant financial statements. The primary adjustment is the change to inventory value on the balance sheet. In the value stream income statement in Figure 6.7, it is clear that the primary reason that net profit was only $99,723 is because of the balance sheet change in inventory. Over time, as Lean reduces and stabilizes inventories, this adjustment will become immaterial for financial reporting purposes.

Standard Costing - Based Income Statement

	Revenue		
		1,039,440	
	Systems	1,009,246	
	Total Revenue	2,048,686	
	Standard Cost of Goods Sold	1,687,800	
	Standard Margin	360,886	
	Adjustments (Favorable) Unfavorable		
	Purchase Price Variance	(59,467)	
	Materials Usage Variance	96,733	
	Labor Variance	(93,895)	
	Overhead Absorption	182,577	
	Total Adjustments	125,948	
	SG&A	135,215	
	Income Before Taxes	99,723	

This standard costing-based income statement shows Cost of Goods Sold at standard based on the products shipped in the period.

All variances are calculated by the ERP system based on the standards set and actual reporting

The standard costing-based income statement is great for financial reporting but poor for operating analysis

Value Stream Income Statement

	OEM Value Stream	Systems Value Stream	New Product Development	Sales & Marketing	Support	TOTAL
REVENUE	$1,039,440	$1,009,246				$2,048,686
Materials	$424,763	$339,810	$84,953	$0	$0	$849,526
Direct Labor	$189,336	$123,648	$0	$0	$0	$312,984
Support Labor	$87,662	$67,616	$40,772	$93,315	$53,056	$342,421
Machines	$88,800	$27,750	$0	$0	$0	$116,550
Outside Process	$36,000	$17,731	$0	$0	$0	$53,731
Facilities	$15,450	$10,300	$3,090	$3,090	$9,270	$41,200
Other Costs	$1,933	$2,899	$483	$2,416	$1,933	$9,664
TOTAL COST	$843,944	$589,755	$129,298	$98,821	$64,259	$1,726,076
VALUE STREAM PROFIT	$195,496	$419,491	($129,298)	($98,821)	($64,259)	$322,610
Return on Sales	19%	42%	−6%	−5%	−3%	16%

Opening Inventory	$1,186,035
Closing Inventory	$963,148
Inventory Adjustment	($222,887)
NET PROFIT	$99.723
	5%

Because the Value Stream Income Statement is based on actual spending, the root cause of spending decisions can be identified and the necessary changes can be make to operations to reduce spending over time.

FIGURE 6.7

Standard costing-based income statement and value stream income statement compared.

WRAP-UP

Your responsibility as Lean CFO is to move your company away from complex cost analysis systems and into value stream accounting. Value stream accounting will allow you to link lean operating practices with financial results and more clearly understand your cost trends. Value stream accounting does this by aligning with the economics of Lean.

Value streams are the true profit centers of your business. Value stream profitability is primarily be driven by delivering better value to your customers, which will drive revenue growth. Your Lean performance measurement system measures how well your value streams are doing delivering value.

The second objective of the economics of Lean is to improve productivity levels to control costs. Value streams achieve cost control by first creating flow and then continuously improving upon it. Reporting actual value stream spending empowers value stream teams to link Lean operating behavior to spending decisions.

Making more money is really no more complicated than shipping more products to customers and spending less money.

As the Lean CFO you must train your company to understand that reducing spending is limited because most of your spending is on materials and capacity. Unless you are a large customer of a supplier, you may not have much control over material purchase price. But you can control material quantities by minimizing raw material inventory and scrap, and thus control spending.

Your company's labor and machine costs are determined by the level of capacity required to meet customer demand. These costs change only when the quantity of total capacity changes. Focus efforts on improving productivity 20% annually, which will control the amount of capacity required and control spending. If capacity needs to be added, it should be because of increasing demand. In this case, the increase in demand will quickly pay for the additional spending on capacity.

By using weekly value stream income statements and measuring kaizen events using the Box Score, your company will have many more "financial analysts" who are in the gemba, taking a proactive role in controlling spending. This sure beats having people analyzing a complex cost report that no one believes.

7

The Value of Measuring Capacity

CAPACITY IN TRADITIONAL MANUFACTURING

In manufacturing, the term "capacity" typically refers to the production capabilities of the factory. Understanding your production capabilities allows you to project the total number of resources (or capacity) required, as well as to measure the effectiveness of those resources.

Traditional manufacturing companies use MRP (manufacturing resource planning) software to calculate their total capacity. A production forecast is input into the software, which uses data such as bills of material and production run rates to calculate material requirements and the number of machine and people hours needed.

The forecast of capacity requirements is important information for you, the CFO, for financial forecasting purposes. Forecasted production hours can easily be converted into production costs, overhead absorption, and variances using your standard costing system.

Traditional manufacturing companies measure the effectiveness of their resources in three ways: the efficiency of labor, the utilization of machines, and how much overhead production absorbs. This information comes from standard costing systems and is based on operations beating the "standard" production rates set up in the system. Labor resources are efficient if they produce at a rate faster than the standard. Machines achieve favorable utilization if actual run time is a high percentage of available time. And all resources are doing well if absorption is greater than planned.

From a financial standpoint, the more favorable the efficiency, utilization, and absorption are, the better the profits are and vice versa. So you pay close attention to these numbers as the CFO. These numbers have a tremendous influence on the financial statements, and often they are discussed more than actual operating numbers. If you have ever been a CFO or controller of a manufacturing company that uses standard costing, you know what a headache these numbers are. So here is the good news: When you become a Lean company, you can throw these numbers away, because they are meaningless to Lean operations.

CAPACITY IN LEAN MANUFACTURING

First, I want to make something very clear. Efficiency, utilization, and absorption measures do not work in Lean companies. They work just fine in traditional manufacturing because they support traditional manufacturing assumptions. But they totally conflict with Lean operating principles. In Chapter 5, you learned that your first job as Lean CFO is to eliminate these measures from your company forever. Your second job is to ensure the integrity of the data used to calculate capacity. Your third job is to integrate capacity into business analysis and decision making.

We've learned thus far that the total resources a Lean company requires are based on a combination of actual demand and the productivity of the resources. Flow and other Lean practices enable operations to maintain productivity levels regardless of the level of demand. This is the reason why Lean companies are less concerned about the total amount of capacity and more concerned with constantly measuring the *productivity* of that capacity.

Lean companies measure the effectiveness of their capacity based on the effectiveness of Lean practices being used. In a Lean company, resources can perform two types of activities: productive or nonproductive. These activities must be viewed from your customers' viewpoint, not from an internal viewpoint. Productive activities are those activities required to create and deliver customer value. These are the activities customers are paying you to do.

Nonproductive activities are everything else. Nonproductive activities can either be pure waste or necessary activities. Waste (such as scrap, downtime, waiting, etc.) needs to be eliminated.

Necessary activities are those activities that a company must perform to support the productive activities (think purchase raw materials) or run the company (think accounting). Customers won't pay you more money if you have best-in-class purchasing and accounting. But they will definitely complain if an order is late because materials are late or their invoice is incorrect. Lean practices must be employed in all necessary activities, just like value streams.

Measuring capacity in Lean companies is really about measuring the amount of time resources spend on productive and nonproductive activities. The best part about measuring capacity is that the information needed is already on the value stream maps.

INTEGRITY OF VALUE STREAM MAP DATA

In Chapter 3 we discussed how value stream mapping is used to measure the waste in a value stream through direct observation of the work being performed. During the direct observation process, the actual cycle times of each process step in the value stream are also collected (Figure 7.1). These data are used to calculate the capacity of a value stream.

I mentioned this in Chapter 3, but it is worth repeating here before we go any further. As the Lean CFO, you must insist that direct observation be used to gather all the operating information for a value stream. Do not allow people to use data from the ERP (enterprise resource planning) system, or let people simply use what their "experience" tells them. This is a critical point, because these data form the foundation for calculating the capacity of a value stream and, as you will learn shortly, will drive improvement efforts.

Figure 7.2 is an example of how capacity is calculated. The total productive capacity of a value stream is its total cycle time multiplied by the average demand. Cycle time is the uninterrupted work time necessary to complete each process step. It does not include any of the Seven Wastes. Average demand is used because producing at a rate greater than demand is waste.

All observations must be done through a "Lean lens," meaning being able to distinguish between a value-added activity and the Seven Wastes.

People without Lean experience may have a difficult time doing this. An investment in some value stream mapping training will do wonders to improve your value stream map data.

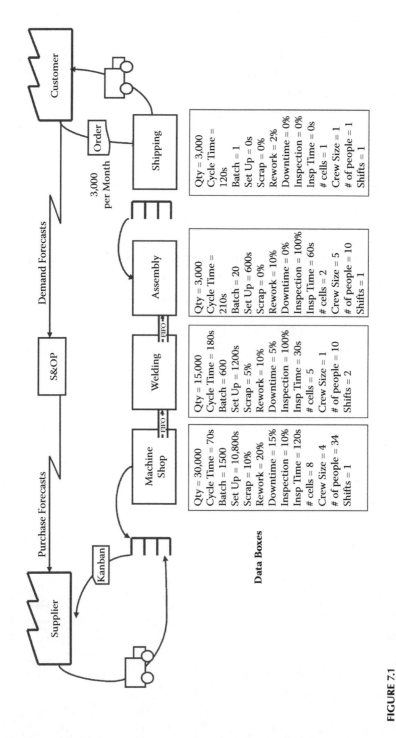

FIGURE 7.1
Value stream map with data boxes.

Machine Shop Data Box from Value Stream Map	Employee Time	Formulas
	Productive	30,000 units * 70 second cycle time * 4 member crew size **= 8,400,000 sec (seconds)**
Machine Shop Qty = 30,000 Cycle Time = 70s Batch = 1500 Set Up = 10,800s Scrap = 10% Rework = 20% Downtime = 15% Inspection = 10% Insp Time = 120s # cells = 8 Crew Size = 4 # of people = 34 Shifts = 1	Nonproductive	Change-Over: 20 * 10,800 = 216,000 sec Scrap/Rework: 30,000 * 30% 70 * 4 = 2,520,000 sec Downtime: 15% * 18,360,000 = 2,754,000 sec Inspection Time: (30,000 + 9,000) * 10% * 120 = 468,000 sec 5S & Clean UP: 600 * 34 * 20 = 408,000 sec Meeting & Reports: 600 * 34 * 20 = 408,000 sec TPM: 1,800 * 20 * 34 = 1,224,00 sec **Σ (all above) = 7,998,000 sec**
	Available Capacity	**Total Employee Time per Month** 34 people * 20 working days * 7.5 hour shift * 3600 sec per hour = **18,360,000 sec** **Productive Time** 8,400,000 sec/18,360,000 sec = 46% **Nonproductive Time** 7,998,000 sec/18,360,000 sec = 44% **Available Capacity** 100% − (46% + 44%) = 10%

FIGURE 7.2
How to calculate capacity of machine shop employees.

The total nonproductive time is total time spent on wasteful activities as shown on the value stream map. The value stream map data for some types of waste are expressed in rates, such as scrap, rework, and downtime. These rates need to be converted into the units of time used on the value stream map. Other types of waste, such as waiting and transportation, are already expressed on the map in units of time. Convert all observed waste into units of time and simply add them up to get total nonproductive capacity.

Productive and nonproductive capacity is expressed as a percentage of total capacity. Total capacity is the total time the value stream resources work in a month. This calculation would be the hours per day that total people (or machines) work multiplied by the number of workdays in a typical month.

Subtracting productive and nonproductive capacity from total capacity will give you the available capacity in the value stream. There are two reasons why there is always some available capacity in a value stream. First, the tools and practices used in a pull system slow down faster processes to work at the rate of the bottleneck, which is the process step with the

> Capacity is calculated from value stream maps and updated when significant improvement events occur. It's not calculated by tracking time.

longest cycle time. Second, Lean companies always reserve a portion of capacity as a buffer for variability that cannot be predicted. This is typically between 10% and 20% of total capacity.

Capacity can be calculated for both people and machines. It's best to calculate capacity based on the resource that is performing the value-added work. The value stream maps indicate which resources are performing this work.

Finally, it's important to remember that there are no "benchmarks" as to what your capacity numbers should look like. You want the current-state capacity to reflect the current state of the value stream accurately based on however much waste really exists. What is important is the trend of capacity numbers over time, which should measure the maturity of Lean practices, improving productivity, and getting better at delivering customer value. Let's look now at specific ways to improve the capacity data.

OPERATIONAL VALUE OF CAPACITY

Establishing flow and continuous improvement eliminates waste. Eliminating waste means operations stops spending time on these activities and literally creates available time. This will be reflected in value

> Once people grasp the concept of continuous improvement, it seems like everyone wants to get in on it. Everybody has lots of ideas for improvement, but not every improvement idea is necessarily a good kaizen event. Here are the two tests to determine if an idea is really a kaizen event:
>
> 1. Would the improvement move the Box Score, and by how much?
> 2. Can someone point to the specific process step on the value stream map that will be improved?

stream capacity measurements as nonproductive time is converted into available time (Figure 7.3a–c). As the Lean CFO, you need to establish the standard work for measuring continuous improvement in your company.

One of the major frustrations of Lean people is their inability to explain to management what a company gains through continuous improvement. Many companies fall back on the "old reliable": cost savings. Some Lean companies have policies in place that require the calculation of cost

		MONTHLY NUMBERS	CURRENT STATE	KAIZEN EVENT PROJECTION
Value Stream Performance Measurements		Productivity (Hrs Worked/Census)	4.89	3.92
		Quality (Defects per Patient Day)	3.20	2.92
		Average Length of Stay (Days)	5.70	4.20
		Patient Satisfaction (0–5)	2.7	3.5
		Average Cost per Patient Day	$192.69	$167.74
		Employee Engagement	33%	37%
Value Stream Capacity		Productive Time %	41.9%	52.4%
		Nonproductive Time %	21.7%	27.1%
		Available Time%	36.5%	20.6%
Value Stream Financials		REVENUE	$332,630	$332,630
		Reimbursable Supplies & Drugs	$56,177	$56,177
		Salaries & Wages	$170,610	$136,488
		Employee Benefits	$53,675	$42,940
		Supplies	$39,862	$39,862
		Drugs	$58,543	$58,543
		Professional Service	$0	$0
		Contracted Services	$0	$0
		Equipment	$6,290	$6,290
		Facilities	$17,482	$17,482
		TOTAL COST	$346,462	$301,605
		PROFIT	−$13,832	$31,025
		Return on Revenue	−4.16%	9.33%
20%		Hurdle Rate	−4%	9%

FIGURE 7.3(a)

Prior to a kaizen event, a Box Score is projected for the event based on the desired outcome of the event.   *Continued*

MONTHLY NUMBERS			CURRENT STATE	KAIZEN EVENT PROJECTION	KAIZEN REPORT OUT RESULTS
Value Stream Performance Measurements		Productivity (Hrs Worked/Census)	4.89	3.92	3.67
		Quality (Defects per Patient Day)	3.20	2.92	2.50
		Average Length of Stay (Days)	5.70	4.20	4.20
		Patient Satisfaction (0–5)	2.7	3.5	3.5
		Average Cost per Patient Day	$192.69	$167.74	$167.55
		Employee Engagement	33%	37%	37%
Value Stream Capacity		Productive Time %	41.9%	52.4%	52.4%
		Nonproductive Time %	21.7%	27.1%	27.1%
		Available Time %	36.5%	20.6%	20.6%
Value Stream Financials		REVENUE	$332,630	$332,630	$332,630
		Reimbursable Supplies & Drugs	$56,177	$56,177	$56,027
		Salaries & Wages	$170,610	$136,488	$136,488
		Employee Benefits	$53,675	$42,940	$42,940
		Supplies	$39,862	$39,862	$39,520
		Drugs	$58,543	$58,543	$58,543
		Professional Service	$0	$0	$0
		Contracted Services	$0	$0	$0
		Equipment	$6,290	$6,290	$6,290
		Facilities	$17,482	$17,482	$17,482
		TOTAL COST	$346,462	$301,605	$301,263
		PROFIT	−$13,832	$31,025	$31,367
		Return on Revenue	−4.16%	9.33%	9.43%
20%		Hurdle Rate	−4%	9%	9%

FIGURE 7.3(b) (*Continued*)
Based on the actual improvements made during the event, the kaizen team creates an actual Box Score at the end of the event. *Continued*

savings to justify continuous improvement activities. Typically, this is done by calculating the amount of time freed up by eliminating waste and multiplying it by some labor or machine rate.

If your company uses this type of cost savings calculation to evaluate continuous improvement, you must insist that this practice end immediately, to be replaced with using the Box Score. Every major improvement activity should "move the Box Score" in the direction of the future state. Most major improvement activities should improve one or more value

| | MONTHLY NUMBERS | CURRENT STATE | KAIZEN EVENT PROJECTION | REPORT OUT RESULTS | KAIZEN OUTCOME | | |
					ONE MONTH LATER	THREE MONTHS LATER	SIX MONTHS LATER
Value Stream Performance Measurements	Productivity (Hrs Worked/Census)	4.89	3.92	3.67	4.00		
	Quality (Defects per Patient Day)	3.20	2.92	2.50	3.00		
	Average Length of Stay (Days)	5.70	4.20	4.20	4.20		
	Patient Satisfaction (0–5)	2.7	3.5	3.5	2.9		
	Average Cost per Patient Day	$192.69	$167.74	$167.55	$171.08		
	Employee Engagement	33%	37%	37%	37%		
Value Stream Capacity	Productive Time %	41.9%	52.4%	52.4%	52.4%		
	Nonproductive Time %	21.7%	27.1%	27.1%	27.1%		
	Available Time %	36.5%	20.6%	20.6%	20.6%		
Value Stream Financials	REVENUE	$332,630	$332,630	$332,630	$332,630		
	Reimbursable Supplies & Drugs	$56,177	$56,177	$56,027	$52,177		
	Salaries & Wages	$170,610	$136,488	$136,488	$140,488		
	Employee Benefits	$53,675	$42,940	$42,940	$42,940		
	Supplies	$39,862	$39,862	$39,520	$41,862		
	Drugs	$58,543	$58,543	$58,543	$58,543		
	Professional Service	$0	$0	$0	$0		
	Contracted Services	$0	$0	$0	$0		
	Equipment	$6,290	$6,290	$6,290	$6,290		
	Facilities	$17,482	$17,482	$17,482	$17,482		
	TOTAL COST	$346,462	$301,605	$301,263	$307,605		
	PROFIT	−$13,832	$31,025	$31,367	$25,025		
	Return on Revenue	-4.16%	9.33%	9.43%	7.52		
20%	Hurdle Rate	-4%	9%	9%	8%	0%	0%

FIGURE 7.3(c) (Continued)

To ensure sustainability of the improvement, the kaizen team reviews the actual Box Score at specified intervals. Deviation from the report out results would be an indication that the improvements have not been sustained.

stream performance measures and convert a portion of nonproductive capacity into available capacity.

Some improvement events will have an impact on value stream costs and this will be reflected in reduction of value stream costs. Because the value stream income statement reflects value stream spending, it is much easier to see the direct impact of the improvement on spending decisions.

The other area where capacity has operational value is in resource planning. Most Lean companies have a 6-month continuous improvement cycle, and they target 10% productivity improvements every 6 months. Because you can calculate future-state capacity from a future-state value stream map, you can easily project operational resource requirements that reflect the productivity improvements.

As the Lean CFO, you can use these resource projections in your financial forecasting. The economics of Lean now become part of your financial forecasts with revenue increasing at a greater rate than costs. This financial trend is supported by the future-state capacity data. They show how your company is delivering more value to your customers without adding resources.

FINANCIAL VALUE OF CAPACITY

Perhaps where the Lean CFO can have the most impact on the long-term profitability of a company is by incorporating the capacity data into the standard work of the financial analysis of business decisions.

The cost of capacity changes only when the level of capacity changes. If available capacity exists and it is used in productive activities, such as meeting customer demand, there is no change in production costs.

If available capacity exists, and there is an increase in demand, the only increase in cost is material cost. The profit the company makes from this increase in demand is the contribution margin of the demand. There is no change in the cost of labor or other production costs because the available capacity exists. Likewise, if demand is increasing and there is not enough available capacity, the cost of buying the capacity must be part of the financial analysis.

This is one important area where standard costing breaks down in a Lean company. If you use a standard product cost to calculate the profitability of anything, you are making the assumption that those costs will be incurred based on each unit sold. Even if you make the assumption that all or a portion of the overhead is "fixed," this still assumes that labor cost will vary with each unit sold, and this assumption is simply not true.

If more capacity is required, it should be apparent by a low percentage of available capacity. Once a value stream determines how many resources are needed, it's quite a simple financial analysis to determine its cost: the cost of the machine, of hiring new full-time or temporary people, or of the number of overtime hours required. None of this is complicated to calculate.

WRAP-UP

Value stream capacity data are the missing link between Lean operational improvements and financial improvement. Most, but not all, Lean practices focus on reallocating resource time away from nonproductive activities to productive activities. This is reflected in improved performance measures, but it does not change the total cost of resources. Value stream capacity measures this change in how resource time is used.

By incorporating value stream capacity into your standard financial analysis, the impact of flow and continuous improvement will be reflected. You will be able to project the true profitability of increasing demand accurately without adding resources.

Now let's look at how we put all the tools together and incorporate the economics of Lean into your company's business decision making.

8

Decisions, Decisions, Decisions

THE CURRENT STATE: STANDARD COSTING AND DECISION MAKING

Standard costing information is still a major source of financial information used to understand the financial impact of business decisions. Since most manufacturing companies use standard costing systems to value inventory, the cost of each product is readily available. Most traditional manufacturing companies consider a product cost accurate. But what is odd is that a great deal of effort is made to ensure this "accuracy": keeping run rates up to date, allocating all production costs, and continuously monitoring actual costs against standard. This leads to a great deal of confidence in using product costs to do financial analysis of business decisions.

Using standard product costs in business decision making works well in traditional manufacturing companies because that is what standard costing systems were designed for. In Lean companies, continuing to use standard costing for business decision making will create conflict and confusion. One of two outcomes can occur when standard costs are used in business decision analysis in Lean companies: Either the wrong decision is made, or traditional manufacturing practices creep back into operations to support the financial analysis.

It's your responsibility as the Lean CFO to remove standard costing information from all business decision making if your company's Lean business strategy is going to have long-term success. This must be done early in your company's Lean journey, because you want to begin organizing business decisions around the economics of Lean as soon as possible.

THE FUTURE STATE: THE VALUE STREAM BOX SCORE AND DECISION MAKING

The three components of a Box Score (performance measurements, capacity, and profitability) are used as the basis for all business decision making in Lean companies. Lean companies understand that value streams generate profits, based on the economics of Lean: delivering customer value and improving productivity. Using the Box Score requires a complete analysis of impact of the business decision on Lean operating performance, which will lead in turn to the financial analysis.

Value stream profitability is based on actual revenue and actual costs. The financial analysis of a business decision is based on the change in value stream profitability over a specified time period: say, 1 month. If future-state value stream profits are greater than today's value stream profits, the business decision makes financial sense.

Financial analysis of value stream profitability must take into account the impact of the business decision on both operating performance and capacity. Box Score performance measures and value stream costs have a direct relationship. Improving performance leads to lower costs and vice versa because the only way to improve all Lean performance measures simultaneously is through flow, pull, and continuous improvement.

The relationship between capacity and value stream production costs is dependent on the amount of available value stream capacity and the amount of capacity needed for a business decision to be enacted. This relationship gets to the heart of the economics of Lean. If a business decision requires more capacity, and the value stream has that capacity available, then there are no additional production costs associated with the business decision. Value stream production costs change only when the level of resources changes.

Let's look at examples of typical business decisions and compare standard costing paradigms to Lean decision making using the Box Score.

USING PRODUCT COST TO SET PRICE

Even though everyone knows that price and cost are not at all related, many companies continue to base pricing decisions on the standard margin of a product. Many companies set policies of minimum standard margins, oftentimes based on financial budgets, in order to analyze the profitability of their products.

Standard margin is used in a variety of ways. One method is simply to set company policy such that a product will be discontinued if it does not have a minimum standard margin. Another method is to calculate the desired price for an individual product from its cost. Linking price to a standard product cost leads to irrational behavior.

Products with margins less than the minimum are often discontinued or outsourced. Unless the lost productive capacity is replaced with other demand, overhead rates will increase, which lowers margins on existing products, which in turn results in more products discontinued or outsourced.

The other typical behavior is to focus on reducing the cost of a product or products. Since direct labor drives product cost, much analysis is done to adjust production run rates, fine-tune labor rates, and reallocate overhead rates. While this work can result in reducing a product cost, it does not change total company costs. Standard costing is a closed system: Changing any part of the system only reallocates costs differently to products and only reallocates absorption and variances. It does not reduce actual costs. The only way to reduce actual costs is to spend less money.

As the Lean CFO, it's your job to bring all of this nonsense to an end. Most sales and marketing people know exactly what price the market will bear. Lean companies develop a deep understanding of the value created by their own products in comparison to those of competitors. Your company will develop this deep understanding of customer value if you focus efforts on improving your company's quality, delivery, lead times, productivity, and flow by 20% per year. Customers usually don't mind the price if they receive the value they desire.

Take a moment now and read Example 8.1, which is a short story that contrasts the use of standard costing and of a Box Score in pricing and profitability decisions.

Example 8.1: The Neutralia Company

Traditional Approach
Joe, a Neutralia sales person, is having a sales call meeting with Karen, the purchasing manager of Axent, a potential new customer. Karen expresses interest in a monthly order of 3000 Pro-Value 602's. Joe quotes the list price of $50 per unit, which has been calculated based on a required 15% margin on a standard cost of $42.34. Karen thanks Joe for the quote and says she will get back to him. Karen calls Joe 2 days later and explains that the $50 price is too high for Axent and tells Joe that Axent's maximum price is $45 per unit. Joe tells Karen he will get back to her.

Profitability Using Standard Cost		
		Quantity
Price	$45.00	3,000
Standard Cost	$42.34	
Profit per Unit	$2.66	
Margin Percentage	5.92%	
Take the Order?	NO	

Joe knows Neutralia requires a minimum of 15% margin on all sales and he will have to turn down the opportunity because the margin is only 5.92%. Joe contacts Neutralia's supply chain manager, Todd, in an effort to find a way to lower the cost of the product to achieve the margin.

Todd gets back to Joe and explains that the supplier of the raw materials will not agree to any purchase price discounts but he did find a supplier who can produce Pro-Value 602's for a lower price than Neutralia's standard cost. The supplier quoted a landed cost of $33.00 for Pro-Value 602's which now generates a margin of 21.17%.

Joe is delighted because he can now take the order and earn an excellent sales commission.

Low Cost Country Outsourcing		
		Quantity
Price	$45.00	3,000
Outsource Cost	$33.00	
Outsource Overhead %	7.50%	
Outsource Overhead Cost	$2.48	
Total Cost	$35.48	
Profit per Unit	$9.53	
Margin Percentage	21.17%	
Take the Order?	YES	

Lean Decision Making Using the Box Score
After Karen's phone call where she requests a $45 price, Joe meets with
Paul, the Pro-Value value stream manager to talk about this opportu -
nity. Paul reviews the current state Box Score with Joe and it shows not
enough capacity to manufacture 3000 Pro-Value 602's per month.

Neutralia Value Stream #1		Current State
Value Stream Performance Measurements	Productivity	$23,087
	On Time Shipment	82%
	Inventory Days	14
	First Pass Quality	88%
	Average Cost	$15.97
Value Stream Capacity	Productive Time %	62%
	Nonproductive Time %	32%
	Available Time %	6%
Value Stream Financials	Revenue	$1,408,333
	Materials	$765,000
	Labor Costs	$267,083
	Machine Cost	$59,433
	Other Costs	$74,233
	Profit	$242,584
	Return on Revenue	$17.2%

Paul tells Joe that by purchasing two new machines and hiring two operators, value stream capacity can be increased to more than the required 3,000 units/month.

Joe and Paul contact Brian, the CFO to prepare a future state value stream income statement which includes 3,000 Pro-Value 602's per month at $45 per unit.

The Pro-Value value stream income statement shows the actual change in revenue and costs associated with adding 3,000 units of Pro-Value 602's per month.

Because Neutralia must purchase additional capacity, labor and machine costs will increase, but the future state return on sales of 20.3% is an improvement over the current state return on sales of 17.2%, which means accepting the order for $45 per unit is a good financial decision.

Value Stream Costing	Current State	New Order	Future State
Revenue	$1,408,333	$135,000	$1,543,333
Materials	$765,000	$52,500	$817,500
Labor Costs	$267,083	$9,476	$276,559
Machine Cost	$59,433	$3,067	$62,500
Other Costs	$74,233		$74,233
Profit	$242,584		$312,541
Return on Revenue	17.2%		20.3%

The value stream now

Incremental costs

The value stream with the Pro-Value 602 order

Box Score Comparison

Neutralia Value Stream #1		Current State	Standard Cost	Outsource	In-House
Value Stream Performance Measurements	Productivity	$23,087	$23,087	$25,301	$23,087
	On-Time Shipment	82%	82%	78%	82%
	Inventory Days	14	14	28	14
	First Pass Quality	88%	88%	82%	88%
	Average Cost	$15.97	$15.97	$16.74	$15.97
Value Stream Capacity	Productive Time %	62%	62%	62%	62%
	Nonproductive Time %	32%	32%	32%	32%
	Available Time %	6%	6%	6%	6%
Value Stream Financials	Revenue	$1,408,333	$1,408,333	$1,543,333	$1,543,333
	Materials	$765,000	$765,000	$871,425	$817,500
	Labor Costs	$267,083	$267,083	$267,083	$276,559
	Machine Cost	$59,433	$59,433	$59,433	$62,500
	Other Costs	$74,233	$74,233	$74,233	$74,233
	Profit	$242,584	$242,584	$271,159	$312,541
	Return on Revenue	$17.2%	$17.2%	17.6%	20.3%

This Box Score compares the three alternatives based on the benefit to the value stream as a whole.

The standard cost decision would not change the Box Score because the order would be denied.

Outsourcing creates a higher cost than making it in the Neutralia factory.
Making it at home is the most profitable decision.

The product cost gives you the wrong answer on profit margins and the wrong answer about outsourcing options.

The right answer comes from addressing the impact on the value stream as a whole.

PROFITABILITY OF NEW BUSINESS

In traditional business decision making, comparing the actual margin of a new order to a minimum required margin is oftentimes the difference between accepting or rejecting new business.

Here is how a new order is analyzed using the Box Score. Obviously, an order will increase value stream revenue. Material cost will also increase based on the volume of material that needs to be purchased. To determine if any other value stream costs will increase, the impact of the order volume on capacity must be understood. If there is enough available capacity to produce the expected volume, there are no additional costs to produce this order. If there is not enough capacity, then the actual costs of the additional capacity must be included in the financial analysis. If the return on sales of the future-state Box Score is greater than that of the current-state Box Score, the business decision makes financial sense. Depending upon the complexity of the decision, the Box Score may look out 1 month, 12 months, or a few years—whatever time frame is appropriate for the kind of decision being made.

DETERMINING THE PROFITABILITY OF CUSTOMERS, MARKETS, AND BUSINESS SEGMENTS

Product costing makes it very easy to look at profitability from many different angles. There are a variety of reasons why these types of analyses are done. You may want to understand how well a part of your business is performing (e.g., "Look how profitable my customers are!"). Or there may be a desire to understand why company profitability is less than desired (e.g., "Which market segment or business units are underperforming?").

Unfortunately, this is not as simple a financial analysis as standard costing makes it out to be. Remember that the financial analysis is on the value stream as a whole. The Box Score analysis begins with understanding the impact on value stream operating performance. As the Lean CFO, you must set up standardized work for decision making so that the people making these decisions take into consideration the following types of questions:

- What is the impact that the demand from the customer or market has on value stream quality, delivery, productivity, lead time, and flow? (If the demand makes value stream performance worse, then there will be a cost impact.)
- How much waste is created in the process due to this customer, market, or business unit?

- What would future-state value stream performance measures be if a particular customer or market segment's demand were removed from the value stream?
- What would we do with any available capacity created by less demand from this source?

Many new business decisions involve more than one alternative, meaning questions similar to the preceding ones must be asked and answered to understand the full impact of the business decision. Example 8.2 illustrates how once these questions are answered, a Box Score analysis will give you the correct information to make the most profitable business decision.

Example 8.2: Calculating the Actual Profitability of New Business

A new customer has approached you to buy & distribute your product in a large new market and wants to pay no more than $15 per unit. They forecast sales of around 14,000 per month, which is about a 20% increase in demand.

The current state box score (Column 1) indicates that there is not enough capacity to meet this demand.

Column 3 is the future state Box Score. It tells us that this is a good decision as profits increase and the value stream improves in performance in terms of productivity, on-time delivery, flow and quality.

	Monthly Numbers	**1** Current State	**2** Impact of the Additional 14,000 Units per Month	**3** WITH NEW DISTRI-BUTION ORDER AT $15 per unit	By working some overtime, we have enough capacity. No more people needed.
Value Stream Performance Measurements	Productivity ($/person in the value stream)	$25,854	$3,443	$29,297	
	On-Time Shipment to Customer Request	82%	9%	91%	
	Inventory Days	14	−6.00	8	
	First Pass Quality	78%	0%	78%	
	Average Product Cost	$17.92	−$1.25	$16.68	
	Employee Engagement in Lean	33%	2%	35%	
Value Stream Capacity	Productive Time %	49%	10%	59%	
	Nonproductive Time %	46%	−7%	39%	
	Available Time %	5%		2%	
Value Stream Financials	REVENUE	$1,577,100	$210,000	$1,787,100	
	Materials	$854,000	$136,640	$990,640	
	Labor Costs	$267,058	$6,980	$274,038	
	Machine Cost	$59,436	$0	$59,436	
	Other Costs	$74,223	$2,400	$76,623	Extra 14,000 units
	Profit	$322,383	$63,980	$386,363	
	Return on Revenue	20%		22%	
28%	Hurdle Rate	−8%		−6%	

The Box Score allows you to do "what-if" analysis to determine the impact on operations, capacity, and profitability.

Continuing this example, this new customer would like to know if you could sell the product to them for $12 per unit, which would increase volume to 28,000 units per month.

Using the Box Score, you calculate that the value stream would have to buy 6 new machines and hire 12 operators to run the machines in order to meet a monthly volume of 28,000 units.

This additional volume at a lower price has a negative impact on volume stream profitability as compared to selling 14,000 units per month at $15 per unit.

	Monthly Numbers	CURRENT STATE	WITH NEW DISTRI-BUTION ORDER AT $15 per unit	If Price Is $12 and Extra Sales 28,000
Value Stream Performance Measurements	Productivity ($/person in the value stream)	$25,854	$27,297	$23,914
	On-Time Shipment to Customer Request	82%	91%	89%
	Inventory Days	14	8	8.0
	First Pass Quality	78%	78%	78%
	Average Product Cost	$17.92	$16.68	$16.34
	Employee Engagement in Lean	33%	35%	35%
Value Stream Capacity	Productive Time %	49%	59%	52%
	Nonproductive Time %	46%	39%	35%
	Available Time %	5%	2%	13%
Value Stream Financials	REVENUE	$1,577,100	$1,787,100	$1,913,100
	Materials	$854,000	$990,640	$1,093,120
	Labor Costs	$267,058	$274,038	$350,240
	Machine Cost	$59,436	$59,436	$79,248
	Other Costs	$74,223	$76,623	$79,023
	PROFIT	$322,383	$386,363	$311,469
	Return on Revenue	20%	22%	16%
28%	Hurdle Rate	–8%	–6%	–12%

OUTSOURCING

In traditional decision making, outsourcing a product is typically based on the price a supplier would charge compared to the product's standard cost. The assumptions are similar to those of discontinuing a product: Costs will be reduced by the standard cost of the product being outsourced multiplied by the annual volume.

Using the Box Score, you can see that outsourcing creates available capacity, and that costs will not decrease unless the value stream capacity is reduced. If the available capacity created by outsourcing is used to meet other demand, there will be no corresponding increase in production costs.

Material costs will go up in a Box Score since the price that the supplier is charging is usually higher than what it cost you to purchase the raw materials. However, there are additional questions to answer: What value are you receiving from the supplier? Is outsourcing improving operating performance? Example 8.3 shows how, by using the Box Score to analyze outsourcing decisions, the financial impact of supplier quality and operating performance can be analyzed.

Example 8.3: Outsourcing Decision

Value Stream Box Score		Current State	Make Product	Outsource to Asia	Outsource Locally
Value Stream Performance Measurements	Productivity ($/person in the value stream)	$29.31	$26.05	$29.31	$29.31
	On-Time Shipment to Customer Request	97.2%	98.0%	95.7%	96.0%
	Inventory Days	8.90	8.50	16.28	10.21
	First Pass Quality	54%	63%	52%	60%
	Average Value Stream Cost per Unit	$111.74	$113.10	$113.90	$112.66
	Employee Engagement in Lean	35%	35%	35%	35%
Value Stream Capacity	Productive Time %	31%	35%	31%	31%
	Nonproductive Time %	56%	62%	56%	56%
	Available Time %	13%	3%	13%	13%
Value Stream Financials	REVENUE	$1,611,456	$1,821,456	$1,821,456	$1,821,456
	Materials	$490,296	$586,296	$575,296	$672,296
	Conversion Costs	$497,933	$527,036	$545,933	$502,254
	Value Stream Profit	$623,227	$708,124	$700,227	$646,906
	Return on Revenue	38.67%	38.88%	38.44%	35.52%

When comparing make/buy decisions, it is important to look at the total impact on value stream performance using the Box Score, rather than simply looking at the price the supplier is charging compared to your standard cost.

This company is considering making a new product in-house that requires a new production process. Making the product in-house will have a negative impact on productivity, but will increase value stream profits.

Two suppliers are considered—one in China and one local. Box Scores are projected based on the total impact on value stream performance. The change in material costs are easy to calculate. What must be considered when outsourcing is the *value* you receive from outsourcing, which is reflected in the performance measures. In the case of either supplier, you won't be receiving much value as on-time delivery and quality decrease and inventory increases.

The Box Score will reveal the correct decision when it comes to outsourcing.

In general, if your company has the capabilities to produce a product to the market's quality specifications, and if you have the capacity to produce the product, then you should make the product in house. This is the business case for in-sourcing production that may have been outsourced in the past, and it should be considered as a way to use the capacity created by Lean improvements. You will improve your quality, delivery, and lead time, as well as reduce costs by in-sourcing.

Using the Box Score to analyze outsourcing prevents the outsourcing "death spiral" that occurs when using standard costing to make outsourcing decisions. If companies set minimum standard margins to determine what to make in house and what to outsource, then all low-margin products will be outsourced. With less production volume, standard costs must increase to continue to absorb overhead. This reduces the margin on more products, which means more outsourcing. Pretty soon there is no volume left in operations, and factories close.

CAPITAL PURCHASES

Most capital purchases are analyzed based on their return on investment. The payback, internal rate of return, or net present value of the investment is calculated to determine if the purchase is financially sound. This is the right way to analyze capital purchases. The issue lies in how the profitability or savings of the investment is calculated. In traditional manufacturing companies, the focus of the analysis is usually on efficiency, absorption, or utilization improvements to determine a level of cost savings or profit increase. From a Lean view, this analysis is not always correct, because cost savings don't necessarily materialize due to these "improvements."

Capital purchases can be easily analyzed through the Box Score. The operational decision to buy a machine means you are buying capacity. This means your projected Box Score should show there is not enough available capacity to meet expected demand. There may also be other operational reasons to purchase a machine, such as improving quality, delivery, lead time, or flow. The projected value stream performance measures should reflect these improvements.

After the operational reasons for purchasing the machine are determined, the financial impact is straightforward. Value stream production costs will increase due to the purchase of the machine, primarily increasing depreciation and possibly even maintenance. However, if the machine is being purchased due to an increase in demand, then the increase in revenue and material cost must be accounted for in the financial analysis. Finally, any improvements in operating performance will have a direct impact on value stream costs. A future-state value stream income statement, with the entire financial impact of the purchase, should be used to calculate the payback, internal rate of return, or net present value.

Example 8.4 illustrates how to use the Box Score for the analysis of capital purchase decisions.

Example 8.4: Purchasing Capital Equipment

	Manual Process	Assisted AL1200A	Semi-Auto Seimens 07	Current Technology CT-120	High Technology CT485	Flow & Place Automation Benis 12	Full Automation CX420
Productivity	6.34	7.05	7.05	7.01	7.94	8.88	7.41
Quality	22%	20%	8%	8%	15%	8%	3%
Length of Stay - Min.	92	92	75	63	69	50	42
Patient Satisfaction	Low	Low	High	Low	Med	High	Med
Average Cost	$322.78	$324.00	$342.37	$338.57	$287.26	$276.52	$406.66
Productive Time	55%	52%	58%	64%	55%	56%	48%
Nonproductive Time	28%	40%	22%	18%	37%	27%	43%
Available Capacity	17%	8%	20%	18%	8%	17%	9%
REVENUE	$4,874,119	$4,474,119	$4,874,119	$5,394,915	$5,394,915	$6,035,895	$6,035,895
People Costs	$1,649,358	$1,483,416	$1,483,416	$1,649,358	$1,457,762	$1,457,762	$1,746,050
Machine Costs	$12,993	$58,933	$125,633	$140,553	$208,645	$487,335	$1,000,255
Supplies & Drugs	$326,844	$399,055	$487,944	$540,080	$602,466	$599,877	$1,186,344
Other Costs	$143,551	$120,544	$125,768	$189,466	$182,433	$340,000	$340,000
Facilities	$812,577	$894,566	$901,344	$900,111	$450,011	$239,655	$322,567
TOTAL COST	$2,945,323	$2,956,514	$3,124,105	$3,419,568	$2,901,317	$3,124,629	$4,595,216
PROFIT	$1,928,796	$1,917,605	$1,750,014	$1,975,347	$2,493,598	$2,911,266	$4,440,679
RETURN	40%	39%	36%	37%	46%	48%	24%

Lean companies do not choose capital equipment and then "justify it."

They use 3P analysis (Production Preparation Process).

The emphasis is on deeply understanding the problem we are trying to resolve, rather than the technology that is available.

Once the problem is clearly understood then the team studies the available solutions.

    – They are required to analyze 7 solutions

    – One solution must be highly manual

    – Another highly automated

    – One uses similar technology to that currently used

Each solution is shown on the Box Score.

HIRING PEOPLE

The traditional view of hiring people is based around payroll costs and head count. The traditional justification for hiring people is about improving efficiency and absorption. MRP may also play a role in hiring operational people because it can calculate total people needed based on a sales forecast and your production capabilities.

Lean companies don't view their people as an expense; they view them as a resource that delivers customer value. The decision to hire people is based on the same operational issue as capital purchases: capacity. In a Lean company, if you flow actual demand, then hiring people is due to an increase in demand. The question that must be answered is whether the demand increase is considered permanent or temporary. Full-time employees are considered permanent demand and should be hired when permanent increases in demand are expected. If demand is considered temporary, then overtime, temporaries, or outsourcing may be sources of temporary demand.

The financial impact of hiring people will be an increase in actual labor costs as well as increases in revenue and margin due to the increase in demand. If the future-state value stream return on sales is greater than the current-state return on sales, and if value stream productivity rates are maintained or improved, then it is a sound financial decision.

Example 8.5 illustrates how to use the Box Score to analyze the financial impact of hiring people.

Example 8.5: Hiring People

		Current: July	August	September	October	November
Value Stream Performance Measurements	Units per person	46.01	44.62	43.15	47.11	51.56
	On-Time Shipment	98.0%	98.3%	99.0%	98.8%	72.3%
	First Time Through	82%	84%	84%	82%	76%
	Dock-to-Dock Days	8.10	8.20	7.60	8.10	3.40
	Average Cost	$263.04	$259.24	$255.83	$250.89	$217.68
Value Stream Capacity	Productive Time %	31%	31%	31%	33%	48%
	Nonproductive Time %	59%	59%	60%	59%	66%
	Available Time %	10%	10%	9%	8%	−14%
Value Stream Financials	REVENUE	$923,974	$895,549	$865,680	$979,075	$1,142,411
	Materials	$317,570	$307,908	$297,735	$336,566	$396,024
	Conversion Costs	$345,084	$330,159	$315,691	$353,259	$378,838
	Value Stream Profit	$261,320	$257,482	$252,254	$289,250	$367,549
	Return on Revenue	28.28%	28.75%	29.14%	29.54%	32.17%

The Box Score projection above shows a temporary increase in demand in November that will require additional capacity.

		Current: July	August	September	October	November
Value Stream Performance Measurements	Units per person	46.01	44.62	43.15	43.99	52.90
	On-Time Shipment	98.0%	98.3%	99.0%	98.8%	99.0%
	First Time Through	82%	84%	84%	85%	85%
	Dock-to-Dock Days	8.10	8.20	7.60	8.10	3.40
	Average Cost	$263.04	$259.24	$255.83	$262.44	$236.83
Value Stream Capacity	Productive Time %	31%	31%	31%	28%	41%
	Nonproductive Time %	59%	59%	60%	49%	60%
	Available Time %	10%	10%	9%	23%	−1%
Value Stream Financials	REVENUE	$923,974	$895,549	$865,680	$979,075	$1,142,411
	Materials	$317,570	$307,908	$297,735	$336,566	$396,024
	Conversion Costs	$345,084	$330,159	$315,691	$362,054	$362,054
	Value Stream Profit	$261,320	$257,482	$252,254	$280,455	$384,333
	Return on Revenue	28.28%	28.75%	29.14%	28.64%	33.64%

Hire 6 additional people in October ⟶

The value stream manager determines 6 temporary people need to be hired in October in order to be trained in time for November. The remaining capacity deficit in November will be made up through over-time.

IMPACT OF CONTINUOUS IMPROVEMENT

In traditionally thinking companies, improvements should yield cost savings. This drives a simple financial analysis: Determine how much time is saved and multiply that by some labor rate to determine the financial impact of improvement. The weakness of this analysis is that cost savings don't materialize, frustrating both executives and leaders of improvement.

In Chapter 7, we learned that most continuous improvement activities create available capacity. Lean companies use this time to deliver more value to customers and improve productivity. Creating time has no direct financial impact on costs, because the level of resources has not changed.

The financial analysis of continuous improvement projects must be based on the change in actual spending in the value stream. Improvement events that focus on the product, such as improving quality, will have a direct impact on material spending. Events that focus on the process, such as reducing setup time, are the events that create time. The actual financial impact of these events depends on what is done with the newly created available capacity.

Three things can be done with available capacity. It can be used to flow more demand through a value stream, in which case the financial impact is more revenue and margin. The available capacity can be reassigned to another value stream, which would reduce the actual production costs in one value stream and increase them in the other. The final option is to reduce the actual level of resources by eliminating the available capacity, which would reduce actual costs. Example 8.6 illustrates how the Box Score is used to calculate the true financial impact of improvements.

Example 8.6: The Impact of Continuous Improvement

			CURRENT STATE	FUTURE STATE
Operational		Sales per Person	$7,472	$7,472
		On-Time Shipment	92%	94%
		First Time Through	71%	78%
		Dock-to-Dock Days	33.0	18.5
		Average Cost	$419.46	$413.97
		Accounts Receivable Days	54.0	50.0
CAPACITY	Employee	Productive Capacity	51%	43%
		Nonproductive Capacity	30%	19%
		Available Capacity	19%	37%
	Machines	Productive Capacity	53%	53%
		Nonproductive Capacity	32%	17%
		Available Capacity	15%	29%
FINANCIAL		Revenue	$332,569	$332,569
		Materials Costs	$111,431	$108,446
		Conversion Costs	$116,753	$116,753
		Total Costs	$228,184	$225,199
		Value Stream Profit	$104,385	$107,370
		Return on Sales	31%	32%
		Inventory Value	$209,336	$113,026
		Cash Flow	$123,117	$288,926

In this example, a value stream created its future state map and future state Box Score, which shows that it will almost double the amount of available capacity when 6 monthly kaizen events are completed. These events will focus on improving flow and quality. How do we know this? These future state performance measures show the most improvement.

But there is little change to the value stream profitability. Material spending is decreased due to the improvement in quality (which reduces scrap). But conversion costs remain the same because creating flow creates more time (and available capacity) but does not reduce costs.

This is how Lean operations "moves the Box Score" with continuous improvement.

But what is the real financial impact of these improvements? That depends on how the capacity is used. Let's look at a few examples.

		CURRENT STATE	FUTURE STATE	TRANSFER TO DIFFERENT VS	IN-CREASE SALES	INSOURCE SUB-ASSY
OPERATIONAL	Sales per Person	$7,472	$7,472	$8,493	$9,904	$7,472
	On-Time Shipment	92%	94%	94%	94%	95%
	First Time Through	71%	78%	78%	78%	78%
	Dock-to-Dock Days	33.0	18.5	18.5	18.5	13.5
	Average Cost	$419.46	$413.97	$399.17	$364.43	$384.07
	Accounts Receivable Days	54.0	50.0	54.0	54.0	50.0
CAPACITY — Employee	Productive Capacity	51%	43%	64%	60%	52%
	Nonproductive Capacity	30%	19%	27%	24%	22%
	Available Capacity	19%	37%	9%	16%`	16%
CAPACITY — Machines	Productive Capacity	53%	53%	59%	69%	69%
	Nonproductive Capacity	32%	17%	19%	20%	20%
	Available Capacity	15%	29%	22%	12%	11%
FINANCIAL	Revenue	$332,569	$332,569	$332,569	$427,938	$332,569
	Materials Costs	$111,431	$108,446	$108,446	$139,545	$92,179
	Conversion Costs	$116,753	$116,753	$108,704	$116,753	$116,755
	Total Costs	$228,184	$225,199	$217,151	$255,102	$208,934
	Value Stream Profit	$104,385	$107,370	$115,418	$172,836	$123,635
	Return on Sales	31%	32%	35%	40%	37%
	Inventory Value	$209,336	$113,026	$51,557	$62,086	$71,131
	Cash Flow	$123,117	$288,926	$125,984	$156,921	$184,263

After completing the future state map it was determined that there were 3 alternatives for using the available capacity created: Transfer people to a different value stream, increase sales and in-source sub-assembly operations previously outsourced. Finance can do complete Box Score analysis by projecting the financial impact of these decisions.

The capacity section of the Box Score shows how the available capacity of the future state is converted into productive capacity due to each of these decisions.

The value stream income statement projects the financial impact of these alternatives. Transferring people to a different value stream will reduce conversion costs and increase the return on sales from 32% to 35%. Increasing sales will increase revenue and material costs but conversion costs will remain the same because there is enough available capacity to meet this demand. Return on sales increases from 32% to 40% in this case. Finally, insourcing sub-assembly operations will reduce material costs while increasing return on sales from 32% to 37%.

It's important for Lean companies to understand the impact of capacity for all business decisions and improvements to be able to project the true financial benefits of Lean.

Lean improvements can generate cost savings only if the level of resources is actually reduced. But the real focus of Lean improvements is to generate capacity to get better at delivering value and growing revenue.

WRAP-UP

Removing standard costing from business decision making can be one of the most difficult challenges for the Lean CFO. How much work this will entail really depends on how deeply embedded standard costs are in your company's decision-making process. Successful business people or companies who have used standard product costs to do financial analysis of business decisions are usually big believers in product costs. Remember that to remove standard costing information from your company's business decision-making system, your primary job is to change the way people think about using product costs.

As the Lean CFO, you need to build new standard work for the financial analysis of all business decisions around the Box Score. The economics of Lean are embedded in the three components of the Box Score. Making the Box Score the required tool to analyze business decisions will unlock the financial potential of Lean for your company. The Box Score will drive consistency in decision making, improve collaboration between departments, and make it easier for nonfinancial people to understand the economics of Lean.

9

Standard Costing Debunked

INTRODUCTION

Standard costing has three primary uses in a manufacturing company: measuring operating performance, profitability analysis, and inventory valuation. In Chapter 5, we learned how a Lean performance measurement system replaces standard costing information, and how measurements such as efficiency, utilization, and absorption are eliminated. In Chapter 6, we learned how to use value stream costing to identify spending patterns and link cost improvement to changes in operating behavior. Finally, in Chapter 8, we learned how to eliminate standard costing from the financial analysis of business decisions by using the Box Score.

That leaves inventory valuation. The Lean CFO understands that standard costing serves one temporary purpose only: to value inventory in a high-inventory environment. Elimination of standard costing is a possibility, but it will be dependent on the rate of reduction in inventory.

A BRIEF HISTORY OF STANDARD COSTING

Standard costing systems rely on entering a great amount of detailed information about production rates, material usage, and manufacturing costs to create standards. Operating performance is measured by reporting actual information against every standard production rate created. The detailed costing information, combined with production information, creates product costs, which are a convenient, simple method for nonoperating people to use to analyze costs at a microlevel, such as product profitability. Finally, using product costs is the simplest and easiest way to value inventory for financial reporting purposes when you have a lot of inventory on hand.

Standard costing works well in mass production manufacturing, because one of mass production manufacturing's operating elements is stability and repetition. Frederick Winslow Taylor's *Principles of Scientific Management* (1911), which formed the foundation for mass production, stressed optimizing and simplifying tasks by using time studies. People are assigned specific tasks, which are designed to take a specific amount of time. Actual times can be compared to standard times to measure operating efficiency. Because inventories in mass production companies were quite large, specific identification of inventory costs became too difficult. That led to the development of standard costing systems to simplify inventory valuation. Since standard costing created product cost information, profitability analysis evolved.

CHARTING THE COURSE TO NO STANDARD COSTS

As the Lean CFO, you must recognize early in the Lean journey that standard costing conflicts with a Lean business strategy. Lean practices wreak havoc on a standard costing system because Lean is all about changing and improving. The only assumptions that hold in Lean are the Five Principles. None of the many assumptions made in a standard costing system are applicable to Lean. The impact of Lean on a standard costing system will be the fluctuation of absorption and variances, which will be even more difficult to explain than before becoming Lean. The reason this will occur is that the rate of change in Lean operations makes the assumptions used in standard costing invalid, and the ability to keep all of the assumptions up to date is an impossible task.

If your company is beginning its Lean journey, you must begin simplifying standard costing systems earlier rather than later because of the impact Lean will have on standard costing. Being proactive in this will prevent a lot of unnecessary work in the future, like trying to answer, "What's going on with standards or variances?" This process needs to be looked at as a journey, beginning with simplifying the system and working toward the goal of eliminating as much of the standard costing system as possible.

Simplifying standard costing systems is related to how your ERP (enterprise resource planning) system uses various pieces of data and information to calculate standard costs. Fortunately, all ERP systems pretty much do this the same way. Standards for production information must be entered into the system. Labor and overhead costs must be calculated and set up. To calculate actual-to-standard information, ERP systems require transactions to record actual information for each standard assumed. The terminology each ERP system uses may be different, but in essence they all work the same way. The design of routers, bills of material, material costs, labor, and overhead rates determines the complexity of a standard costing system.

SIMPLIFYING MATERIAL COST

Material cost is developed from the bills of material. There are four factors that create complexity in material costs: the number of bills of material, the parts on bills of material, the quantity used of each part on bills of material and the material cost per unit (Figure 9.1).

Bills of material must be created for any product that gets recorded as completed production in an ERP system. This means that all your finished goods, as well as any subassemblies that get recorded into stock as completed production, must have bills of material. In traditional manufacturing, subassemblies are typically produced independently of the finished good of which they are a part. These subassemblies have their own bills of material. The bill of material for the finished goods will have on it all subassemblies taken from stock, as well as other raw materials consumed.

Bills of materials	Traditional drivers of complexity	Lean drivers of simplicity
Number of bills of material	Number of unique items reported as subassembly and finished goods inventory	Finished goods only
Number of line items	Number of items reported as raw material and subassembly inventory	Purchased parts only
Unit of measure	Number of inventory items with bills of material drive multiple conversions	One conversion
Quantity per assembly	Costing, absorption, and forecasting	Actual quantity

FIGURE 9.1
Simplifying bills of materials.

In Chapter 3, we learned about single piece flow and pull systems. These Lean practices will eliminate the need for subassemblies to be stocked as inventory, which means they don't have to be reported as completed production. The bills of material for subassemblies can be eliminated in pull systems. A typical first goal is for the number of bills of material to match the number of finished goods that a company sells.

It is also possible to reduce the number of bills of material further. Some ERP systems have "configurable" bills of material, which are created (a one-time configuration) for customized products as the material is consumed during production, which would be appropriate for a highly customized manufacturing environment. Another feature is allowing the substitution of parts on existing bills of material. In both cases, it's possible to use system features and have even fewer bills of material on file.

Traditional manufacturing companies like to list every possible part, no matter how large or small, on bills of material. The reason for this is for variance analysis, inventory control, and purchasing purposes, but doing this creates unneeded complexity in material costs. Every part listed on a bill of material must have a quantity used. For discrete parts, should the quantity used be the actual quantity used to produce the product? Or should it include a yield rate, which is the scrap rate? Including yield rates "helps" for inventory control purposes, but creates complexity in costing. Even more difficult are "parts" that are really consumable supplies, such as paints and powders. The quantity used is often difficult to measure (e.g., "Who really knows exactly how much paint is used to coat a product?"). In a Lean company, the pull systems in place on the shop floor and with suppliers will regulate the quantity of material purchased and used. There is no need for ERP systems to track everything and determine when parts and supplies need to be ordered. Bills of material can be simplified by eliminating small parts, such as screws or difficult-to-measure ingredients. Treat these items as shop supplies.

To get operating performance information, actual material information must be recorded to get variances. Purchase price variance (PPV) requires each part received to be entered as well as the actual invoice price. Material usage variance requires actual material consumed to be reported at each production step. Because Lean companies use a Box Score, this work can be eliminated.

Traditional companies spend a great deal of time determining the "standard" material cost to enter for each purchased part. This is the primary reason that so much effort is made to measure purchase price variance.

Some companies keep it simple: They enter the price the supplier charges. Other companies try to get creative by entering the price they would like to pay, so that the effectiveness of the purchasing department can be measured using PPV. In some cases, determining the purchase price is difficult. One example is commodity prices, which fluctuate frequently. In other cases, suppliers may change prices without warning. Lean companies recognize that PPV is a meaningless measure. Simply cost material by always using the last price paid as the "standard."

The goal here is not to make material costs more accurate, but rather to simplify the process to reduce the amount of nonproductive time that goes into maintaining material standards. Reduce complexity by reducing the factors that impact the standard material cost: the number of bills of material, the level of part detail on bills, and by trying to define the standard unit cost. The goal is for material costs to be reported at actual cost.

SIMPLIFYING LABOR AND OVERHEAD COSTS

ERP systems calculate labor and overhead costs by assigning labor and overhead rates to work centers, and by creating routings for each product that is reported as completed production. The complexity in labor and overhead costs depends on the detail level of work centers, the number of routers, and the level of detail in labor and overhead costs (Figure 9.2).

First, all possible production steps in the factory must be laid out in the ERP system. These are typically named work centers or process steps in ERP systems. Next, routers are created that link each product to specific

Routers	Traditional drivers of complexity	Lean drivers of simplicity
Number of routers	Number of unique items reported as work-in-process and finished goods inventory	Finished goods only
Line items	Number of production process steps and costing accuracy	Number of value streams
Run rates	Costing, absorption, and forecasting	Cycle time
Labor and overhead rates	Product cost accuracy	One each per plant

FIGURE 9.2
Simplifying routers.

work centers to map the actual production process steps for each product. The term *router* simply means the route that the product takes through the production process. Like bills of material, each product that gets reported as completed production—all finished goods and all subassemblies that have inventory locations—must have a router.

Each step on the router must be given a run rate, which is the time it takes to complete one unit in that process step. Determining the run rate is very similar to determining the quantity of each part on a bill of material. For certain work centers, especially machines, the production cycle time is easy to determine. In other work centers, the production cycle time can vary due to a variety of issues, which can occur at any time. This is often the case when labor is involved. One simple example would be the case of a more experienced worker being able to assemble a product at a rate 20% faster than an inexperienced worker. What is the correct run rate to use?

Run rates are used to calculate variances and absorb overhead costs. Actual times must be entered for each step on a router for the system to calculate the variances. The system calculates absorption by multiplying the quantity of completed production by the run rates. Some companies, in an effort to absorb more labor and overhead, inflate the run rates to include such activities as machine changeover time.

The typical approach when standard costing is a primary provider of performance information is to have as many work centers as possible to develop detail routers, so that the system can track production, and to measure and adjust run rates constantly to maximize absorption. This system requires actual information to be recorded against each production step on work orders.

Labor and overhead rates are developed for each work center based on how costs are assigned or allocated by the cost accounting function. Some of these costs are easy to identify, such as how many people work in a work center. Most of the costs are difficult to assign specifically to work centers. This is where cost allocation systems are used. The traditional approach is to develop complex allocation schemes to assign as many costs as possible so that the system can create an "accurate" product cost, which can in turn be used to understand the profitability of products. Even in a standard costing environment, this level of detail gets way beyond inventory valuation and has a tremendous impact on business decision making, which we discussed in Chapter 8.

What you learn about your operations when you adopt Lean practices is that there is variability. Some of the variability is the result of the way you have designed the production process, and other variability is beyond your control, such as the rate and mix of demand. The role of Lean is to do two things simultaneously: Strive to eliminate the variability that you are capable of eliminating (continuous improvement) and manage what you can't eliminate with flow and pull. The end result is that operations are in a constant state of change.

Creating flow is really redesigning production processes based on Lean practices. Many times this means that current work centers will be combined, eliminated, or sequenced differently. Continuous improvement will have an impact on the cycle times to complete a production step and the number of people needed in a production step, as well as eliminating downtime and changeover time. This means that today's physical layout and work activities will not be the same in a few months. This makes it very difficult to keep detailed work centers and routers up to date.

Step one for labor and overhead cost simplification is to minimize work centers and routers as much as possible. As opposed to a work center for every production step needed in making a product, create one work center for each value stream. Simplify routers by having as few steps as possible on the routers. This will reduce the number of transactions that must be entered into systems.

Pull systems regulate both production and inventory in a value stream. Every resource in the value stream knows through visual signals what needs to be worked on and when. Pull systems eliminate the need for detailed tracking of the movement of materials through production in ERP. Simplified routers eliminate a great deal of tracking transactions for both material and labor. The minimum amount of quantity information ERP systems need to know is the quantity of finished goods completed. The calculation of actual labor time can be stopped immediately because all it does is create labor variances.

Step two for labor and overhead cost simplification is to reduce cost allocations and the number of labor and overhead rates. If inventories are greater than 30–60 days, you will probably have to maintain your standard cost system to capitalize labor and overhead. But you won't be using product costing for financial analysis and won't be using variances and absorption for performance measurement. In this case, minimize cost allocations and have one labor rate and one overhead rate for each plant.

Flat bills of material, minimal work centers, one-step routers, and single plant-wide labor and overhead rates will greatly simplify your standard costing system, while still allowing you to use it to value inventory. This work can literally begin on day 1 of your company's Lean journey. By simplifying standard costing, you will be eliminating a tremendous amount of waste in your finance processes, and you can reallocate this created capacity toward Lean accounting efforts.

ELIMINATING STANDARD COSTING

The capitalization of manufacturing costs into inventory causes the most problems on the financial statements because of its impact on reported profits.

The more inventory a company has and the more that production rates don't match shipping rates, the more complex this issue becomes. The typical result is that reported profits don't make any sense when compared to shipments, and/or margins don't make sense based on product mix. The typical solution is to throw more resources at the standard costing system: more detailed reporting, more detailed design, or more analysis.

Generally accepted accounting principles (GAAP) require inventory to be valued at actual cost, but GAAP does not require that each individual product in a business be assigned a standard cost. Standard costing is a system designed to approximate actual, but requires constant adjustment. If a company is audited, auditors test its standard costing system; if it approximates actual inventory, it is considered to be valued accurately. If it does not pass the auditors' testing, the auditors will require the company to capitalize a portion of its variances for inventory to approximate actual for audit purposes.

Lean practices eliminate these problems. Make-to-order and flow will minimize finished goods inventory, and valuing it for financial reporting purposes becomes less material to the financial statements. Production rates match shipment rates. This creates the opportunity to simplify the capitalization of labor and overhead costs.

The Lean solution is to capitalize labor and overhead costs at a macro-level rather than product by product. This meets all GAAP requirements and can be accomplished with a simple journal entry at month end. The magic number is about 30 days of finished goods and work-in-process inventory on hand. If your company has about 30 days of inventory, it was produced during the month. The value stream income statement for the month will list the actual production costs for the month. The amount of production costs to capitalize will be the ratio of goods on hand to total production for the period. The journal entry simply adjusts the previous month's capitalized costs to the current month. Figure 9.3 illustrates an example of how to use a value stream income statement to capitalize inventory with a simple journal entry.

The primary issue in valuing work-in-process inventory is determining the percentage complete so that the proper amount of labor and overhead

			Quantity Produced	Cost per Unit
Step 1: Calculate Actual Cost per Unit for Period	Revenue	2,048,686		
	Material	849,526	22,861	37.16
	Conversion Costs			
	Direct Labor	312,984		
	Support Labor	342,421		
	Machines	116,550		
	Outside Processing	53,731		
	Facilities	41,200		
	Other	9,664		
	Total Conversion Costs	876,550	22,861	38.34
	Total Costs	1,726,076		
	Value Stream Profit	322,610		

	Ending Inventory	Quantity	Material Value	% Complete	Conversion Value	Total Value
Step 2: Calculate Ending Inventory and Change in Inventory	Raw Materials	11,430	424,739	N/A		424,739
	Work in Process	3,430	127,459	50%	66,753	193,212
	Finished Goods	4,753	176,621	100%	182,230	358,851
	Ending Inventory					976,802
	Beginning Inventory					(1,186,035)
	Change in Inventory					(209,233)

		Debit	Credit	
Step 3: Adjust Balance Sheet Inventory	Inventory		209,233	
	Cost of Good Sold	209,233		

FIGURE 9.3
Simple inventory valuation method.

is capitalized. This is the reason companies with high work-in-process must report production against work orders.

In Lean companies, the pull system reduces and limits the amount of work-in-process on the factory floor. If your production cycle times are short, don't bother valuing work-in-process except maybe at year end. Value your work-in-process inventory as if it was raw materials or finished goods. This is possible because the amount of capitalized labor and overhead on a small amount of work-in-process is immaterial for financial reporting purposes. If your production cycle times are long, as in weeks, you can use a simple assumption that all work-in-process is standard percentage complete.

Using this method to capitalize labor and overhead allows you to change your labor and overhead rates to zero, which will make the system-calculated variances and absorption numbers vanish. Combining this with changing material cost to last price paid will generate actual inventory numbers.

This method to capitalize production costs into inventory will meet all audit requirements. The method described here is really the weighted average method to value inventory, which is one of three methods described by GAAP. The other two are first in/first out (FIFO) and last in/first out (LIFO), which really become irrelevant as inventories are reduced. Auditors are very receptive to this method of inventory valuation because it meets GAAP requirements and greatly simplifies the audit process.

WRAP-UP

It is possible to eliminate standard costing from your business. How fast? That depends on how effectively your company deploys Lean practices. If your company truly commits to establishing flow and all other Lean practices, inventories will be reduced dramatically over time. Then, valuation of inventory for financial reporting will become immaterial.

Think of the amount of work that goes into calculating standards, reporting actual, analyzing variances, and explaining the differences. This is all pure waste, and it can be eliminated once and for all from your business.

10

Tame the ERP Beast

INTRODUCTION

Enterprise resource planning (ERP) systems are an integral part of every manufacturing company. Every employee, at some level, uses the ERP system, whether to process transactions, record information, or just read reports. The daily functioning of your company is totally dependent on your ERP system. Think about how many times work stops when "the system is down."

ERP systems are information beasts (Figure 10.1). They are designed to collect and report unlimited amounts of information based on how a company designs the setup of the software. All ERP systems are designed on traditional manufacturing management practices.

ERP systems are designed to *plan the execution* of manufacturing operations. They are designed and configured based on how a factory is supposed to run. As much operational transactional information as possible is recorded and then complied and reported to management, who use this information to run the business and make decisions (Figure 10.2). Data are more visible across the organization and are available very quickly. Transactions and data are analyzed, and control is maintained.

ERP AND THE CFO

As a CFO, you have a major stake in your company's ERP system. Your financial reports are produced from the general ledger maintained in the ERP system. The source of much of the general ledger data comes from operations' reporting of how it executes work. Revenue recognition is

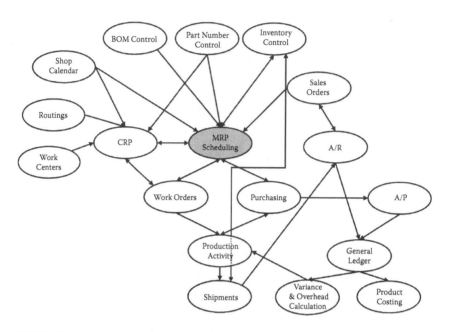

FIGURE 10.1
Typical ERP system flowchart.

dependent on which products are made and shipped. Inventory value is based on properly recording material transactions. And if you use an ERP-based product costing system, then variances, absorption, and cost of goods sold are all based on work order transactions. Proper control of these transactions is essential to accurate and reliable financial statements.

In traditional manufacturing companies, finance and operations agree on the need and uses of ERP. Traditional manufacturing operating practices use ERP to schedule and plan the execution of work, track inventory, and report operating performance. Reporting the execution of work in ERP creates the transactions that give both operations and finance the information it needs for control and reporting.

As a Lean CFO, you must recognize early in your company's Lean journey the impact that Lean operating practices will have on your ERP system. First, Lean operating practices have less reliance on ERP than traditional manufacturing operations. Second, if your ERP system was designed and configured for traditional manufacturing practices, it will impede flow if it is not changed. Third, Lean practices will reduce inventory and the need for complex inventory accounting in ERP.

The good news is that these issues do not have to be dealt with all at one time. Lean practices take time to mature, which gives you time to work

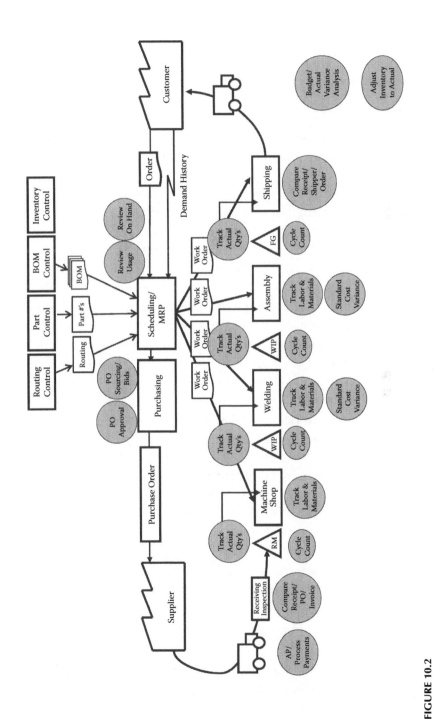

FIGURE 10.2
ERP transactional controls necessary in traditional manufacturing.

with operations to develop and implement a plan to tame the ERP beast and make ERP work with Lean, rather than against it.

LEAN OPERATIONS AND ERP

A Lean operating system is a real-time execution system. It is proactively designed to flow actual demand as fast as possible through value streams. Flow is actively managed and maintained visually by the people in the value stream. What needs to be worked on can be seen, and interruptions to flow are made apparent immediately and dealt with rapidly.

In Chapter 4, we learned how the various Lean practices and tools are used to create a pull system to flow demand and maintain productivity. The rules of the pull system virtually eliminate the need for ERP control of Lean operations. Regulating production, such as exactly which product is to be worked on next, is done with visual cues for each operation step in a value stream, eliminating the need for work order control of production.

Inventory quantities can be controlled through a combination of Lean practices. First, all inventory is visible and at the point of use in the value stream. Second, single piece flow is used between production steps if possible. Third, if true flow cannot be established, kanban levels in supermarkets are used to regulate production and limit inventory. The impact on inventory is to reduce the quantities to the consistent kanban levels. The quantity of inventory can be calculated based on kanban levels. There is no need to track inventory movement through the production process because it doesn't vary unless kanban levels change.

To summarize, Lean practices totally control operations from the point material is received from suppliers through to when finished goods are shipped to customers (Figure 10.3). The mature Lean plant needs two ERP transactions: material received and finished goods shipped. All transactions occurring between these two transactions can be eliminated, but

ERP systems cannot actively manage operational variability, they cannot identify root causes of waste, and they cannot solve problems. Only people can do this.

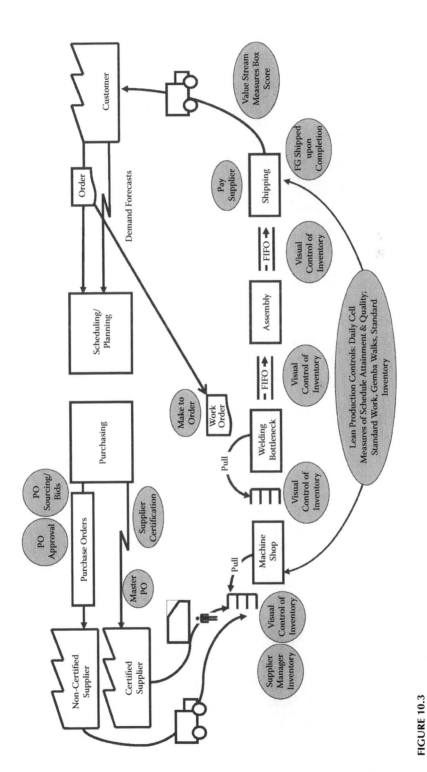

FIGURE 10.3
Lean controls that replace the ERP transactional controls.

only when Lean practices are in place and effective. Let's look at how you, as the Lean CFO, can create a plan to eliminate most shop floor transactions over time.

THE LEAN CFO AND WORK ORDERS

ERP system design usually requires work orders to be closed for manufacturing so that the system can convert all raw materials and components into finished goods, which must be in the system for ERP systems to ship and invoice product.

As a Lean CFO, you need to focus on minimizing the number of transactions that need to be made against work orders, because every work order transaction is waste in operations. The goal is for one work order transaction to be done upon the shipment of the product so that the system can ship and invoice properly. But you probably can't go from recording every work order transaction to recording only one transaction in just one step. That is where back-flushing comes in, which is a feature in most ERP systems.

Back-flushing is a method to designate which work order steps must be reported as completed. Most systems only require the first step (release the materials) and the last step (report completed finished goods quantity) to be reported. It is optional which steps in between are designated as reporting steps.

When pull systems are initially started, it's possible to reduce the number of reporting steps easily by implementing back-flushing. As pull systems mature and flow improves, you can migrate toward reporting only the first and last steps. In addition, the number of work order steps can be reduced as flow increases (see Chapter 8).

WORK ORDERS AND WORK INSTRUCTIONS

A common reason used not to reduce or eliminate work orders is that work instructions are often printed on work orders. The Lean solution to this is visual standard work for each work step.

You can spend millions of dollars and thousands of hours designing an ERP system to track and value inventory better, or you can invest the thousands of hours and little money in reducing inventory using Lean practices and never have to worry about inventory again. Which gives you a better return on investment?

THE LEAN CFO AND INVENTORY QUANTITY

From your Lean CFO perspective, you need accurate inventory in order to value the inventory properly.

In theory, ERP systems should do a great job of keeping track of the quantity of inventory. In reality, this is not the case. Keeping the system quantities accurate requires transactions to record every movement of material from receipt through each production step to shipment, as well as transfers between locations. The result is that oftentimes the quantity shown in the system does not match the physical quantity because of improper or untimely reporting of transactions. Blind reliance on inaccurate system quantities leads to improper purchasing habits, rescheduling of production, and other wasteful activities.

The inaccuracies in system quantities lead to the creation of another nonproductive activity: cycle counting. Cycle counting is supposed to correct all of these inaccuracies, but, in reality, it only compounds them. With cycle counting, you are trying to get a good count while production and reporting transactions are ongoing. The only time you can be assured that system quantities and physical quantities match is if production ceases and inventory can be counted (such as during physical inventory).

As a Lean CFO, you can leverage the benefits of your pull systems to make counting inventory easier. Pull systems reduce inventory quantities to the maximum kanban levels, which are calculated by operations based on average demand and flow. So at any point in time, you know the maximum inventory quantity. The actual quantity on hand can be observed visually on the shop floor. It's quite easy for operations to count the actual kanban levels at the close of a period and then simply make necessary adjustments to quantity on hand in your ERP system.

The level of maturity of the pull system will determine the rate at which transactions can be eliminated, and then you can move to the counting system described in the previous paragraph. The two key measurements to determine the maturity of the pull system are material flow (inventory days or turns) and average order fulfillment lead time. In general, the higher the material flow and the lower the lead time are, the more transactions you can eliminate. However, the one caveat, which may limit your ability to eliminate transactions, is the actual production cycle time.

For example, if your company has about 30 days of inventory on hand and an average lead time of less than 1 week, it would be easy to count inventory when needed. This would be true in a high-volume factory that makes consumer products. But if you are a low-volume factory (say, making airplanes) and production cycle time is weeks, then it may be easier to use back-flushing to get inventory quantity.

Pull Systems create additional benefits beyond calculating inventory quantity. Less inventory and fewer inventory locations will reduce inventory adjustments. Mature pull systems can also eliminate the need for cycle counting and/or complex year-end physical inventories.

Your responsibility as Lean CFO is to determine the leanest, least waste-generating method to calculate inventory quantities when needed. You must also determine how often you need the exact quantities on hand. This depends on the materiality of your inventory. If quantities are not material, can you simply use the maximum kanban levels to estimate and periodically do counts? Or are there specific business reasons that actual quantities must be reported each month?

THE LEAN CFO AND WORK-IN-PROCESS VALUATION

ERP systems are designed to do value work-in-process inventory at a very detailed level, but they require entering quantities completed against work orders. From a Lean operating view, these transactions are unnecessary. As a Lean CFO, you don't want to force wasteful transactional work on Lean operations.

If your work-in-process quantity is low and stable, does it really make a material difference to the financial statements if work-in-process is 50% complete or 65% complete? If the answer is no, then use an average percentage complete. This works well in both high-volume environments with short production cycle times and low-volume environments with long production cycle times.

If you are considering getting a new ERP system and you are on your Lean journey, look 3–5 years ahead when designing and configuring ERP.

WRAP-UP

Your job as the Lean CFO is to tame the ERP beast. Decrease transactions over time so that the information flow doesn't interrupt the material flow. This will also minimize the nonproductive time of transaction processing for operations. Taming ERP will also reduce the level of confusing and complex anti-Lean information that ERP systems can produce.

Early in your company's Lean journey, team up with operations to develop a long-term plan to reduce and eliminate transactions based around the effectiveness of Pull Systems. Make your ERP system work for Lean rather than against it.

11

By the People, for the People

If you would ask experienced Lean people what the key is to making Lean successful in any company, you will get one answer: people. Success with Lean comes from employees building Lean practices, using them, and improving them everywhere, every day, all the time. The same is true for a Lean Management System.

Every employee in your company will be using the Lean Management System. As the Lean CFO, it's important for you to involve employees in the development, deployment, improvement, and sustainment of your company's Lean Management System. Doing this will ensure that every-one has an ownership stake in the system, and it will become "theirs" rather than "Accounting's."

Over the course of my 20-year career in implementing Lean Management Systems, both as a CFO and as a consultant, I've found that the way you approach a Lean Management System and how employees perceive your approach are often the difference between success and failure. So here are some tips.

SYSTEM THINKING VS. PROJECT THINKING

CFOs with education and work experience based in accounting have a tendency to think "short term, project based." Don't take this the wrong way; it's a product of our work environment. Your focus is on work such as the month-end close cycle, preparing an annual budget, completing an acquisition, or a particular financial analysis. Everything you work on has a starting point and an ending point.

A Lean Management System has a beginning, but it has no end. Once the system is up and running, the work is not over. It has to be improved over time. Adjust your thinking to "long-term systems thinking." This will allow you to create and articulate the vision for your Lean Management System.

As a Lean Management System is deployed, the employees using it begin to think that simply recording and reporting the Box Scores is the "work" they must do. With your system-thinking view, you will be able to move your company beyond this and into the *application* of the Lean Management System throughout the business.

ALL EYES AND EARS ARE ON YOU

I'd like to make this perfectly clear: You cannot simply pay lip service to principles of Lean, to the economics of Lean, or to Lean practices. You must totally believe in each of them and be 100% committed to their implementation and development in your business. Anything less than this will impact how employees view Lean and the Lean Management System.

Employees of a company listen to every word that management says (and doesn't say). They also watch facial expressions and body language. You can't fool them. They quickly figure out when words and actions conflict. If you are not committed, they will quickly determine that a Lean Management System is just another "flavor of the month" idea of management that will go away once the next idea comes along. When employees sense your commitment, it will make them inquisitive and want to learn more. This is because Lean and a Lean Management System are so different from what you do today. Also, Lean practices and the information used in a Lean Management System make a lot of sense to your employees. I can't tell you how many times I've heard employees say, "We should have done this years ago!"

KEEP IT SIMPLE

Anyone who doesn't have practical experience with Lean and a Lean Management System can get lost very easily in the details. Most of your employees are inexperienced when it comes to Lean. Keep your message principle based rather than tool based, and give your employees a chance to learn Lean.

People learn Lean by doing it. Yes, training is important, but employees will learn much more by practice. A principle-based message allows employees to connect "why" a Lean Management System is necessary and "why" change must occur.

The Five Principles of Lean explain what a business will focus on and how it will operate. The economics of Lean explains in simple terms how Lean makes money. Once employees make these connections, half the battle is over.

STICK TO THE PLAN

The purpose of this book has been to give you a blueprint for designing, constructing, and using a Lean Management System. Sure, your company's specific plan may have its differences with what I've laid out. But it will work as long as the plan is based on Lean principles, the Economics of Lean, and systems thinking. There may be some stumbles and setbacks, and the original plan may need some tweaking, but it will work.

Allow the Lean Management System to evolve over time, based on improvements from those using the system. I've seen companies who think they have to get a Lean Management System "right the first time"; otherwise, it's a failure. Remember that the majority of your employees have no experience with a Lean Management System, and the company will get better at it the more you use it.

Don't allow short-term business issues to interfere with the design or construction of the Lean Management System. I've seen companies commit to a Lean Management System and begin to develop and deploy it, only to stop it as soon as the first business crisis comes along. Some companies never go back to it because there is always another crisis. Others eventually decide to pick up where they left off, only to find out that this really means starting over from the beginning. This behavior will confuse your employees. They will not know what you are really committed to.

BELIEVE

Believe in your employees—period. You need them to help you design, construct, and use the Lean Management System. But they have no experience with this. They have to learn while doing, which makes for a "sloppy" process involving stumbles along the way. But in the long run, they will get it.

Be positive. Show unwavering support. Celebrate learning, rather than just success. We learn from our setbacks.

And most of all, make it an enjoyable experience for everyone.

Index